The 401(K) Revival

Using Professional
401(k) Management to
IMPROVE PERFORMANCE
and MINIMIZE LOSSES

The 401(k) Revival –*Using Professional 401(k) Management to Improve Performance and Minimize Losses*

Copyright © 2021 by Michael Watkins

First Edition 2021
Published by: Tampa Bay Advisory, LLC
172-A State Street East, Oldsmar, FL 34677
www.401KRevival.com

Written by: Michael Watkins |
mwatkins@tampabayadvisory.com

Library of Congress Case
Watkins, Michael
The 401(k) Revival - Using Professional 401(k) Management to Improve Performance and Minimize Losses
Case Number: 1-10152572551 | February, 2021 | Literary Work

Library of Congress Cataloging-in-Publication Data

ISBN: 978-1-7377906-0-0

Category: 401 (k), Financial, Money Management

Edited by: www.TheWritingProfessor.com

Format & Prepared for Publication by: Eli & Jahshua Blyden |
www.EliTheBookGuy.com

Printed & Published in the USA by: A&A Printing & Publishing |
www.PrintShopCentral.com

Disclaimer

This book is for information and educational purposes only. All information is believed to be accurate at the time of its publication. Individual financial needs differ from person to person and each individual should consult with a knowledgeable professional for all legal, tax, and financial dealings. *The Author, Publisher,* nor Editor make no claims or guarantees in this book. This book is intended to help people think about their financial future and make forward looking decisions in an **attempt** to better safeguard their 401(k) savings and other investments. Common *sense* and practical use of safe money principles are encouraged for everyone. ***The author believes*** 401(k) <u>investors</u> should seek professional help to actively manage their accounts on a daily basis in an attempt to side-step market crashes and improve performance.

The 401(k) Revival

Preface

"The sky is filled with stars, invisible by day"
– Henry Wadsworth Longfellow

The Investment World is moving at lightning fast speeds which could spell big trouble for the traditional 401(k) *"Buy and Hold Strategies."* There is no reason why the next generation of 401(k) participants should risk losing half of their savings like the baby boomers did early in the 21st century. Advancements in technology are helping money managers better protect 401(k) plans from severe stock market losses. I believe the next wave of 401(k) investors who take their wealth building seriously and pay careful attention to market risks have the opportunity to significantly outperform the previous buy and hold investors.

Your retirement might seem a long way off, but every systemic shock *(Severe Stock Market Loss)* you suffer will proportionally impact your ending balance. Severe market losses destroy the rhythm of compounding which robs you of valuable time. Losing valuable time is horrifying when you think about it because time waits for no one.

Over the last decade there has been a silent movement inside the 401(k) world to usher in better tools to help plan participants compound their savings in more efficient ways.

Having a watchful guardian standing by to react quickly and respond to adverse situations on your behalf might be something you have dreamed about. As you have heard before, dreams can come true.

Implementing strategies to side-step severe stock market crashes is the most important thing 401(k) plan participants can do to protect their wealth. Remember, every systemic shock your portfolio suffers is a major blow to your life savings which will further reduce your retirement lifestyle proportionally. Warren Buffet, the famous investor, says *"Never go backwards."*

Professionally, I help pre-retirees carefully design their retirement dreams on paper. Far too often, I have seen a reoccurring theme. Some retirement savings portfolios have been woefully inadequate to support the type of retirement lifestyle these hard working people had envisioned. I have witnessed first-hand folks' disappointment when they learn the cost estimates for their retirement dreams are not matching up with their account balances. Getting to the end of your working career and discovering your retirement lifestyle dreams are not realistic is something I want to help you avoid.

Because I have shared many uncomfortable and heartbreaking moments with clients, I feel it is my moral and fiduciary responsibility to help improve the outcomes for as many 401(k) participants as I can. I want to help you stay on the right side of the market. Building a winning formula for your retirement savings is all about assembling a winning team dedicated to your success. Let your 401(k) Revival begin NOW!

The 401(k) Revival

Table of Contents

The 401(K) Revival

Using Professional 401(k) Management to IMPROVE PERFORMANCE and MINIMIZE LOSSES

BY MICHAEL WATKINS

The 401(k) Revival

Introduction

You can't cross a sea by merely staring into the water.

– R. Tagore

Participating in an employer's 401(k) plan has been a great savings tool for hard working Americans. The employer's payroll process does all the heavy lifting for you and there is no need to shoulder the incredible discipline it takes to save on your own. Month after month, employees make contributions, and in many cases, employers will match a certain percentage of the employee's contribution or salary. This type of steady and timely savings contribution is the foundation for achieving a secure retirement.

News Flash! The income generated by the traditional tax deferred 401(k) plan is now being targeted as another major source of tax revenue by federal government. With 28 trillion dollars of debt, we have reached a tipping point that even our elected officials can no longer ignore. Consumer and Income taxes will most likely start to climb, but that may not be enough to reconcile our massive debt.

The deal we made when we signed up for a 401(k) account allowed us to fund the account with nontaxable dollars from our paychecks. We also get a tax deduction for making those contributions. There is also a very clear rule we all MUST follow! Taxes WILL be payable in the future, upon distribution, at an UNKNOWN tax rate.

As horrifying as this may sound, it gets even worse. There are new rules tied to our government health care system that will affect the amounts and types of income you may have saved for retirement. Exceeding certain limits will trigger a huge penalty or surcharge. Surcharge is a politically correct name for TAX.

The government run Medicare you and I were counting on in retirement is now going to be much more expensive for the middle and upper middle-class income earners. Why? The new Medicare surcharge thresholds have been substantially lowered to funnel in much needed tax revenue. The more retirement income generated from tax deferred dollars the higher your health coverage will be. In fact, I have calculated the surcharges, and in some cases, there is a potential for the entire Social Security Benefit check to be consumed by these new rules.

Take Courage! The IRS is going to come to your rescue. Yes, you read that correctly. The IRS is going to be your hero. If your current retirement savings strategy is full of tax deferred assets generated through *401(k), 403(B), and 457 employer sponsored plans* you will need to make sweeping changes to your retirement plan or face major penalties in the future. Re-allocating future income into the proper tax classifications will avoid these severe tax burdens.

There is another critically important issue you must address now to ensure your retirement savings can remain unscathed by a stock market crash or multiple crashes before you retire. Over the last twenty years, two stock market crashes have taken a major bite out of the 401(k) plan participants' savings—*approximately 50% in losses for most plan participants during that time frame.* The absolute worst part of these crashes was not losing the money itself, but rather the staggering twelve years it took to fully recover from those very painful losses. Think about being robbed of the ability to grow and compound your savings for twelve long years.

401(k), 403(B), or 457 plan participants must avoid severe stock market losses now and in the future if they want to fund a carefree retirement life that may last 20 plus years. A large number of Baby Boomers had their retirements torn in half from 2000-2009 and some are still working today as a result of those losses. Those who were not able to continue working had to adjust to a lifestyle of living on less. Living on less in retirement is not what most folks would consider ideal. Severe stock market losses would devastate your financial future, but I will show you how to avoid a substantial portion of a severe market crash.

Missing the worst days of the market could save you more than you think; it could save you years of catching up. With Fiduciary investment advice and *Stop-Loss* asset protection, your account can be professionally managed (based on your risk tolerance). Adjustments can be made to your portfolio on an as-needed basis and according to Morningstar™ the managed account solution utilized by individuals generated an annual income that was 56% (net of fees) more during retirement compared to those individuals using prepackaged accounts.

You will notice throughout this book that there are quotes from Warren Buffet and Albert Einstein. By design, these quotes are repeated often to help you focus on financial principles that are critical to your financial success and longevity. After all, your end goal is to fund the longest vacation of your life *(Retirement)*, and aren't vacations supposed to be fun and carefree?

The fast paced world we live in today is full of noise and conflicting information. However, there is a quiet confident space occupied by those money savvy folks who do not follow the retail strategies of the masses. These people are risk averse and they understand how devastating losing money is to their retirement savings.

They also understand that paying close attention to tax laws can also give them more income in retirement. This is a badge of honor those folks will proudly wear into a future that could potentially see post World War II income tax levels. Though it lasted fewer than four years, World War II was the most expensive war in United States history. Adjusted for inflation to today's dollars, the war cost over $4 trillion dollars. By the end of 2021, the CBO says our national debt will exceed 30 trillion dollars. Researching the history of income tax rates in the U.S. from its inception in 1913 to today could give you some insight. Preparing for an unknown tax future is potentially the biggest decision you will ever make.

In full disclosure, I am an Investment Adviser Representative with Horter Investment Management and Principal of Tampa Bay Advisory, LLC. I help people all over the U.S. take control of their employer sponsored plans every day. By correctly positioning their 401(k) accounts, they can relax with confidence knowing they have the ability to sidestep severe stock market crashes. I also help people rescue their orphaned accounts left behind at previous employers. Not paying attention to these left behind accounts could be one of the biggest financial mistakes people are making today. Many people are unaware how much better their retirement life will be by rescuing these accounts from high fees and market volatility.

Whether you are starting on your career path or near the end of that journey, having the ability to sidestep the large majority of a stock market crash could save you a significant amount of stress. It could also save you valuable time and money, and aren't those things worth saving?

Just imagine how you would feel if you were able to sidestep a severe market crash or even multiple crashes before and after you retire. If your goal is reaching a stress free retirement, welcome to my world. This is my passion and what I love doing. It's revival time!

CHAPTER 1

It's Revival Time

*Everything that exists in your life does so
because of two things:
something you did or something you didn't do.*

–Albert Einstein

The word **Revival** has a few different meanings. One is *a highly emotional religious gathering* and another is *a new presentation of something old.* The 401(k) Revival is a new presentation of something old that has been highly emotional for many people. The underlying theme of The 401(k) Revival is to help educate you and build confidence in using proven investment strategies inside your 401(k) account.

The 21st century is evolving rapidly with stunning advancements in technology being made daily. In the last decade, computerized and math-based trading has started to dominate the market. The practice of high-frequency, algorithmic trading to identify beneficial trading arbitrage and opportunities is becoming increasingly popular in today's fast-paced market.

There are many underlying factors that have investors worried. There are the geopolitical risks of not knowing what is going to happen next. Worries if there will be another war breaking out and the markets crashing as a result for example. There are concerns of inflation. Government debt has reached horrifying levels. Some investors are worried about getting stuck in a bond bubble with the uncertainty about interest rates changing. There is a lot of uncertainty and nervousness.

To further complicate matters, investors are facing obstacles like the rise of computerized trading and volatile equity and bond returns on investments. It's becoming harder and harder to identify opportunities for diversification. A more active investing approach with the goal to minimize losses and maximize gains would certainly help. By utilizing a math-based strategy to identify risks and forward looking opportunities, investors can smooth out volatility and enjoy more gains and fewer losses.

Investors are no longer trading or investing in the market based on fundamentals, technical analysis, or chart reading. They are competing against a machine; a machine running complex and numerous algorithms every second. This current market structure positions everyday (401(k) investors) against highly sophisticated trading systems.

How in the world can an individual with a day job adequately compete against this type of Wall Street technology? And how well do you think a buy and hold strategy like owning a basket of mutual funds will hold up to blazingly fast market movements. Imagine competing against a system that can buy and sell based off a few words from individual statements made throughout the day? These advancements continue to accelerate year over year and if you are not prepared to compete with this new sophisticated technology, you may be left behind.

The fear and anxiety of having large chunks of your life savings disappear in a few years or in less than a month, like what happened in March of 2020, can be upsetting, stressful, and physically draining. 401(k) plans were originally designed to be set up and left unattended with no oversight or management. Keep in mind this type of strategy was designed over 40 years ago. In a fast paced environment, daily oversight and management is critical to any market driven savings strategy. The biggest danger today's 401(k) investors face is not having the ability to side-step market crashes quickly. Minimizing large losses is the key to building significant wealth inside a 401(k) plan or any other investment. Remember, the less you lose the more you get to keep.

Today's 401(k) plans are simply sitting ducks bobbing around in a sea of extreme volatility. There is nothing standing between an unmanaged account like the 401(k) and financial ruin.

Is there anyone looking out for your financial best interest? Are you in a position to take defensive measures during a stock market crash?

Millions of Americans participating in an employer sponsored plan have somehow accepted taking on these extreme risks without any type of warning system. How would you feel about losing a significant portion of your retirement savings similar to what happened in 2000-2003, 2008 and 2020? The answer is obvious, but a better question might be how you would feel about losing a significant portion of your savings when you knowingly could have prevented it.

> The late great *Jim Rohn* famously said,
> *"You don't know what you don't know ...*
> *And sometimes what you think you know really isn't so"*
> Physiologist *Claude Bernard* also said
> *"It is what we think we know already that often prevents*
> *us from learning".*

It's impossible to know everything there is to know and a good deal of what we think and believe can be the result of influences. Perhaps by parents, teachers, family, friends, co-workers, or even talking heads on T.V. Sometimes we may absorb marketing that has a biased slant to it. Sometimes inaccurate or bad advice seems to makes its way into our lives. Usually, it is not by malicious people, but rather by uniformed well-meaning people. It's funny how folks hear something repeated over and over and then they start to believe it themselves without investigating the facts. Then, these well-meaning folks sometimes pass on what seems to be sage advice for others to use.

Just think back to a place and time in your life when an idea or belief you had been holding on to was rebuffed. Or perhaps it was altered by the discovery of new information. Life is full of ebbs and flows and many things can and do change as we make our way through life. I too have learned from many experiences along the way. Today, I am much better informed than I was yesterday, last week, last year, and last decade.

Our curiosity and human desire to improve prompt us to absorb new information, ideas, and strategies as we evolve. No longer do we or should we rely on everything we have been told or think we know from the past. Our curiosity sparks us to look for better ways to do things and after all, we are living in the information age where information flows to us freely at no cost.

If we query "Investments" in Google, we receive over 2 billion results in less than a second! What do you do with all that information?

Have you ever discovered that, after spending many hours of research online, what you were looking for happened to be right around the corner? I have experienced that little miracle from time to time myself. It simply illustrates that in a world of what seems to be endless options, sometimes we can find exactly what we need close to home.

In a financial world full of impressive pie charts, graphs and statistical theories, sometimes the human element gets lost. What many of us really want is someone who we feel is listening to our story, our concerns, and possibly our deep seeded fears of the Money Monster. Many times, our fears can come from a lack of understanding especially when we journey inside the very foreign world of financial mumbo jumbo and complex marketing brochures.

Today, we often hear the term influencers. What is an influencer anyway and what is their purpose? An influencer is someone who has the power to affect the purchasing decisions of others because of his or her authority, knowledge, position or relationship with his or her audience. Currently, 3.5 billion people actively use social media - that's 45% of the world's population. Today, we can find knowledgeable resources all over the planet, but in the end, it all comes down to preference and our comfort level of who we decide to work with.

We may ask ourselves, do I try to build trust in my financial dealings with someone many miles away or should I take the more human approach by engaging with someone near me? I'll suggest you can do either because I have. It all boils down to your comfort level, intuition, and discernment. Some of my most transparent and rewarding business relationships have been formed through phone conversations and in virtual settings. I may never meet some of my clients face to face, but we always get there by using technology. Being able to see each other as well as exchange information and ideas virtually is not only convenient, but it is a tremendous time saver.

Today is an amazing and wonderful time to be alive. Never before have we had so much knowledge at our fingertips. But applying the right information in the correct manner best suited for our personal goals is another story altogether and quite frankly it can be difficult to get right. We need solid leadership and counsel in this area if we want to keep up with the financial world of the 21st century. Times are changing rapidly. And 401(k) savings strategies designed over 4 decades ago are not prepared to keep pace with today's technology.

The 401(k) Revival is going to challenge you to try something new and exciting in an effort to better manage your 401(k) plan. Taking the first step in any new direction may feel uncomfortable to you and understandably so. My desire is to help you accumulate significantly more wealth than you would have the ability to do with a pre-packaged 401(k) plan. I also want to help you avoid the financial disaster of a severe market crash or multiple market crashes and keep your winning streak going. Staying on the right side of the market is where we need to be if we are going to have a shot at a carefree and stress-free retirement life.

A NEW day has dawned for 401(k) investors! No longer do you have to struggle with managing something as foreign and complicated as your 401(k) investments.

Let your Revival begin now!

CHAPTER 2

The Big Switch

The past cannot be changed.
The future is yet in your power.

— Hugh White

The origins of retirement plans date all the way back to the Ancient Roman Empire. Rome started offering pensions to retiring soldiers during the first century B.C. which initiated a long tradition of military pensions. However, the spread of pensions to the civilian workforce in the U.S. did not gain popularity until the 19th century. In 1875, The American Express Co. created the first private pension plan in the U.S. for the elderly and workers with disabilities.

These early pensions were designed to pay out a relatively low percentage of the employee's pay at retirement and were not designed to replace the employee's full final income. However they set the table for the future of pension plans in the U.S. The American Express Companies forward thinking and thoughtfulness of their employees' well-being after their service to the company was a good start towards our modern 21st century retirement plans.

Fast forward to just after World War II when all the brave men and women returned home from overseas wars. America's large corporations were competing for top talent by offering their employees pensions (Defined Benefit Plan) and other incentives. That phenomenon was a dream comes true for "The Greatest Generation." Suburbia, the Middle Class, and Baby Boomer generations were born and life was really, really good.

The big promise of the day was if you work hard and show loyalty to a corporation, the company would take care of you in your old age. The promise to provide a livable income in retirement was a dream come true for millions of Americans. Sadly, the enormous burden corporate America boldly shouldered in the 1950's, and 60's started to unravel on their "Baby Boomer" children in the late 1970's. The great corporate pension experiment ultimately proved too costly to maintain for most businesses. As inflation slowly crept its way into the 70's and corporate earnings started to slump, the writing was on the wall for the private pension plans future.

The 1970's brought staggering inflation, disco, and legislation that changed retirement forever. In 1978, Congress passed The Revenue Act of 1978 in which Section 401(k) cleared the way for the establishment of defined contribution plans to replace the pension plan. A defined contribution plan takes its name from the ability of the employee and/or employer to contribute a fixed sum to the plan. Over time, different types of plans evolved to serve different types of employees: 401(k) plans for the private sector employees, 403(B) plans for nonprofit and public education employees, 457 plans for state and municipal employees, and Thrift Savings Plan (TSP) for Federal employees.

Three years later in 1981 the IRS issued rules that allowed employees to contribute to their 401(k) plans through salary deductions which jump-started the widespread roll-out of 401(k) plans in the early 1980's. By 1983, nearly half of all large companies offered or considered offering a 401(k) plan and corporate America liked this option too because it was cheaper to fund than pensions. Employees were also attracted to the new savings vehicle that, they were told, could put them in a better financial position to retire. "The Big Switch" was now underway and this new experiment like its predecessor the "Pension Plan" started with lots of fanfare and enthusiasm. Thanks to the two bull stock market runs in the 1980's and 1990's, 401(k) accounts soared higher and there was excitement in the air. Real excitement!

Then two recessions in the 2000's erased those gains and left investors bewildered and fatigued. Still there was confidence in knowing you could automatically have a payroll deduction taken directly out of your paycheck before taxes and receive a tax deduction. In many cases employers would make additional contributions which was a real boost and sign of good will towards the employees. So in just over 40 years the citizens of the United States witnessed one of the best private wealth building experiments of modern times.

The Pension Plan in the early 1950s leveraged the employee's trust and reliance on a corporation's ability to properly manage a large pool of money to fund the employee's income in retirement. The Pension Plan Model got off to great start until outside forces contributed to its demise. The big winners in this experiment were clearly "The Greatest Generation".

The 401(k) plans concept is brilliant when you think about it and with the IRS allowing for automatic payroll deductions in 1981, the 401(k) plans were in vogue all across America. This one act removed the burden and discipline for employees to save independently. The ease of automatic payroll deductions became the fuel that helped explode this new wave of retirement savings that millions of Americans were so eager to participate in. The option for an employer to make contributions also helped to accelerate the savings process and incentivized employees to work hard and stay the course with that employer.

Employers loved the 401(k) plan because of the role it plays in employee retention. Employee satisfaction is a key component to keeping their top talent from leaving for a position with a competitor. The 401(k), 403(B), and 457 plans offered the employees a savings opportunity they would be hard pressed to effectively do on their own. This type of forced savings has dramatically improved the employee's retirement outlook and it has given Middle America a shot at a more dignified retirement.

CHAPTER 3

A Better Understanding

"Perfection is not attainable, but if we chase perfection, we can catch Excellence".

— Vince Lombardi

The 401(k) plan and its equivalents are some of the greatest wealth building concepts of all time. They have done a very respectable job in helping Americans save for a better financial life in retirement. We are so fortunate to live in this great nation. The American dream is based on our freedom to work hard, build wealth, and create a better life with hope and financial security for our families. The 401(k) plan gives millions of Americans that opportunity.

There are pros and cons to most everything in life and the 401(k) plan is no exception. Today, more and more employees are investing in their future through their employer sponsored 401(k) plan. Some employees are even taking their involvement a step further by doing their own research and re-arranging the funds within the plans core line up in an attempt of maximizing performance.

When directing your investments, you will need to consider the investment objectives and risks to return characteristics as well as their performance over time. Understanding the investments inside your plan is the key to making sound investment decisions. There are many online platforms to gather research and data from such as Morning Star that rate the mutual funds using a "Star Rating" for simplicity. As described via Morningstar.com® website, "Morningstar is an online platform where investors can find the latest information and analysis on investments like, Mutual Funds, Stocks, Exchange Traded Funds (ETF's) and Bonds. They even have a learning center *"investing classroom"* and a fantastic Investing Glossary for further explanations."

During the beginning years of the 401(k) plan, internal fees were very high and largely went unchecked until recently. Because of tremendous competition in today's financial world, even the Wall Street giants have been forced to lower fees. Today, many plan providers point out their low fees. Often times that water can be a bit murky and according to SmartAsset.com, the national average of annual fees inside 401(k) plans is 2.22%. That seems pretty reasonable when you consider that some plans have all in fees as high as 4%.

The contributions to the account along with earnings on your investments will increase your balance over time. However, internal fees and expenses paid by your plan may substantially reduce the growth in your account which will reduce your ending balance and retirement income proportionally.

As a plan participant, you may welcome the variety of investment options and the additional services, but you should also be fully aware of their cost. Knowing how fees affect your retirement savings is important. Let's take a look at some of the basic types of fees and expenses.

Plan Administrative Fees: These fees are for day to day administration expenses, recordkeeping, accounting, reporting, compliance testing, and electronic access to your plan account. A third party administrator **(TPA)** is generally responsible for these duties. The third party administrator relieves the employer of many burdensome day to day activities and their fees are usually passed on to the plan participant. Again, all fees are baked into the 401(k) cake, but as you can see there is a lot of heavy lifting going on to maintain compliance and ease of access for you the plan participant.

Sales Charges (aka loads and commissions) This expense may be paid when you invest in a fund which are commonly known as **front-end-load.** The front end load is deducted up front and therefore reduces the amount of your initial investment. When you sell an investment product, the expense is known as **back-end-load, deferred sales charge,** or **redemption fee**.

12-B1 Fees: These fees are considered to be an operational expense of the mutual fund itself and it is generally between .25 and .75%. This fee is simply what you pay to have access to the mutual fund. Think of it as a rent payment. Some funds may advertise "no-load funds". This can mean there is no front-end or back-end load. However, there may be 12B-1 fee.

Investment Fees: By far the largest component of 401 (k) plan fees and expenses is associated with managing plan investments. Fees for investment management are generally assessed as a percentage of assets invested. Your total net return is your return after these fees have been deducted. When you look at your daily ending balance, that number is net of fees.

Passive Management: Generally, these plans have lower management fees. The plan participant chooses a basket of mutual funds based on their risk tolerance and generally it's left unattended unless you change your risk tolerance. This strategy is based solely on the performance of the mutual funds inside the plan and takes no measures for protecting against market crashes or major corrections. This strategy is strictly a set it and forget it approach and is the most widely use strategy in America. As the market goes, so goes your account balance with this strategy.

Quarterly Rebalancing Management: These investment managers will generally reallocate funds on a quarterly basis by adding better performing funds when the underperforming funds reach a certain threshold. This form of Active Management is considered by some as a better approach than the set it and forget it strategy. With this type of money management, your account is being monitored and adjusted on a quarterly basis. This strategy attempts to improve gains, but typically has no safety mechanism to sidestep market crashes.

Daily Management: Daily management is a high level of money management. The idea of using an active money management approach is to minimize large downside losses and maximize upside gains. Watchful daily oversight during market trading hours allows money managers to make swift adjustments when needed. Using sophisticated computer algorithms, these money managers are well equipped to protect your investments from catastrophic losses like in 2000 and 2008 and again most recently in 2020. Having the ability to side-step market crashes can dramatically improve your wealth accumulation.

In addition to the above mentioned there are other fees that can be charged for other services like Target Date Funds, Collective Investment Funds, Variable Annuities, and Stable Value Funds.

Please note that fees are customary on all types of investments and should not necessarily be viewed as bad. However, there can be excessive fees being charged in some plans and those fees should be addressed.

> For the Passive Management (*set it and forget it*) .5 to 1% in fees is acceptable.

> For Quarterly Rebalancing Management 1-2% in fees is acceptable.

> For Daily Money Management 2-3% is acceptable.

The famous Investor **Warren Buffet** has two powerful rules for investing.
Rule #1: *Never lose money*
Rule #2: *See rule #1.*

Albert Einstein said Compound Interest is
"The Eighth Wonder of The World"
Those who understand it,
earn it... those that don't pay it!

Lost Opportunity Costs is a term used to describe the aftermath of a severe stock market crash. If we look back at the start of year 2000 the market dropped three straight and painfully slow years. It took an additional four years to fully recover for a total of 7 years of lost opportunity costs. Then we experienced the 2008 crash and it took an additional 5 years to fully recover totaling a staggering 12 years of lost opportunity in the first decade of the 21st century. This time period has been termed "The lost decade" inside the investment world.

Over those 12 long years of recovery, the internal cost inside the 401(k) plans continued to erode their balances even further. These losses are more damaging to a retirement account than most folks realize. This type of wealth erosion along with the staggering losses suffered inside these accounts is why some people were forced to continue working in order to save more for their retirements.

Lost opportunity cost is a direct violation of Warren Buffet's Rules for Investing and Albert Einstein's theory on Compound Interest. Having the ability to Sidestep the worst stock market days is the real Key to investment success and building wealth. There is a rhythm to compounding and when it gets interrupted for extended periods of time, the magical power of compounding is lost.

Remember, the stock market is cyclical. Market drawdowns can be very destructive to a portfolio's performance, especially because on a percentage basis, you must earn more than you lost just to get back to even.

The Mathematics of Losses & Gains

If a $10,000 investment loses X%, how much in gains are needed to break even?

% of Stock Market Losses	Value Remaining after Loss	Gain % Needed to Break Even
10%	$9000	11%
15%	$8500	18%
20%	$8000	25%
25%	$7500	33%
30%	$7000	43%
40%	$6000	67%
50%	$5000	100%
60%	$4000	150%

In addition to the hidden fees and lost opportunity cost created by severe market losses, there are also mistakes being made by a participant's lack of investing experience. Untrained investors trying to manage their own accounts can and do make some bad choices. And as a result of their frustrations, many continue to repeat those same bad choices again and again.

Your financial wellbeing and retirement income will be based on how well your investments perform today. The chances of the average investor being highly successful managing a 401(k) account are stacked against them to begin with. What if a major stock market collapse begins? Would they have the wherewithal and ability to respond appropriately?

More and more employers are seeking the help of Fiduciary Advisors to help teach the importance of risk management to their plan participants. By doing so the employee wins and the business owner wins. When plan participants stay on the right side of the market year over year, they remain happy and the employer's fiduciary liability shrinks. I believe a happy employee becomes a more productive and loyal person. For many business owners, keeping their key employees happy is a large part of their financial success. The 401(k) Revival helps you magnify that success.

There is some very concerning news everyone participating in an employer sponsored plan should take seriously. John Bogle, the founder of the famous mutual fund, Vanguard, says we should prepare for at least two declines of 25%-30% or maybe even 50% in the coming decade. So, the founder of Vanguard is telling us we are going to lose money. That is very bad news for the buy and hold strategy most 401(k) investor's use.

We know it's coming. We just don't know when and how severe it will be or how long a recovery or multiple recoveries could take. What if it takes another 12 years just like it took in the beginning of the new century? That's over

25% of a 40 year working career and it would be a devastating blow to anyone's ending balance. How you structure and manage your 401(k) today will determine if you will have enough income to live on tomorrow. Leaving your hard earned money in the hands of fate is a huge gamble and it's one you cannot afford to lose. Warren Buffet says *"failing to plan is planning to fail"* This book is all about winning. Winning comes from surrounding yourself with professionals who view your success as their badge of honor and highest priority.

The stock market is risky enough for professional investors let alone novice investors. Using a buy and hold strategy without proper oversight, may open you up to serious consequences if you get caught inside a major downturn or bear market. When the stock market goes up, even mediocre investments will rise with the tide. Getting caught inside a bear market is what you want to avoid at all costs. Building significant wealth is not a game for amateurs to experiment with because your financial future and retirement wellbeing is at stake.

Retirement goals are a very personal aspect of financial planning for which individuals tailor their savings and investments. This makes a great case for utilizing a managed account solution opposed to guessing or asking a co-worker for advice. The bottom line is if you use a buy and hold strategy, doing so without professional oversight and *Stop-Loss* protection is a very risky endeavor. At the very least, (in my humble opinion) every 401(k) plan participant should install an early warning system so they can potentially save a major chunk of principal when the next market crash happens. Today there are new options available to 401(k) investors that can substantially reduce losses and maximize gains. Without the use of modern technology and active management overseeing your retirement plan you could experience the same financial setbacks that tore millions of 401(k) accounts in half at the beginning of the century.

CHAPTER 4

Looking Back to The Future with Vance Howard of Howard Capital Management

"The belief in a thing makes it happen"

– Frank Lloyd Wright

The year 2021 is the most exciting time to be alive in human history. We are living in the most medically advanced times and the quality of life is getting better each and every day on so many levels. Science has discovered new ways to help us improve the quality of our lives and who would have thought almost everything we need to ward off disease and live a healthy life already exists here on earth. The advent of the computer has accelerated much of this research and the computer has also given us new and amazing powers to analyze and discharge information in the blink of an eye.

In the investment world, technology has made giant leaps forward in stock trading and money management. Many people are accumulating tremendous wealth because of it. I have interviewed Mr. Vance Howard of Howard Capital Management, Inc. so you can learn more about this modern-day trailblazer in the 401(k)-money management space.

Michael Watkins – Vance, let's begin this chapter with a brief bio so the readers can get a better understanding of who you are and how your company helps folks better manage their money.

Vance Howard – *Well, I started in this business back in the 80's. And one of the key things I learned back then was you need to stay on the right-side of the market. That is how we started developing the HCM-Buyline® proprietary system.*

Being proactive with risk management is the backbone of Howard Capital Management. Everything we do has to be derived by math. There cannot be a group of guys in here guessing at this. We're in the odds business. We're not in the guessing business.

The backbone of our firm is the HCM-BuyLine®. The HCM-BuyLine® has never sat through a bear market. In 2000, 2002, we sidestepped roughly 95% of those bear markets and we virtually sidestepped all of 2008. I think we were down all of a point and a half and that was net of fees. And within two weeks of coming back into the market in March 2009, all of our clients were back to hitting new highs in their accounts. So, risk management is paramount to us and is also one of the backbones of our proprietary mutual funds and ETFs.

We started Howard Capital Management around 1999 and began lining up selling agreements with different RIA's and Brokerage firms. We're mainly a money management trading firm on behalf of clients and advisors around the country – that's what we have developed over time.

We developed the 401(k) Optimizer® to help advisors and clients manage their 401(k), 403(B), and 457 plans. Recently, we have taken the system a step further and are now offering 401(k) Optimizer® Guided Retirement, an automated, managed account solution. We've partnered with FIS Relius, a recordkeeping software company and our partnership allows us to actually trade the account on behalf of the client and bill fees out of the account, so we're compensated to do so.

We've also developed a high-net-worth division. If you have a million dollars or more to invest, we provide a white glove treatment. We help many small-, mid-, and large corporations.

We have a lot going on at Howard Capital Management. Again, the backbone of our theory is math. Everything has to be based upon math. And even when we allocate money, we're not guessing at the most interesting asset class, whether it's biotech, energy, small capital, large cap, international, etc. It all has to be based upon math. We believe math is going to place us in the most productive asset class on any given stretch.

Michael Watkins – So Vance, in the book, I talk about one of the biggest stumbling blocks of wealth building and how severe market losses create lost opportunity for the consumer. Can you comment on that and how that affects people's portfolios?

Vance Howard – *Not only does it ruin their long-term returns, Michael, but it also is incredibly stressful. It brings a tremendous amount of stress upon the physical body of the person. In 2008, when people had lost 30, 40, even as much as 50 or 60 percent of their investable assets, it was horrifying.*

And as you know, if you lose 50 percent of your money, you need a 100 percent return just to get back to even. For some, it's taken 5, 6, 7, 8 years to get back to even. And of course, many sold out at the bottom because they couldn't handle the stress of it all which compounded the negative effect on their account.

We saw this in 2000 and 2002, with that nasty bear market, it was a slow, grinding, painful market. I remember it vividly. But we were sitting in short-term bonds and cash and we weren't making as much money, but we weren't losing anything. Of course, 2008 was a straight down market with banks imploding, which was pretty terrifying in and of itself.

And then, of course, the pandemic, with the HCM-BuyLine®, we caught that turn pretty much spot on. We were out reasonably early. But also, the good thing about the HCM-BuyLine® is it's mathematically driven. So, it pulled us back into the market and we were able to pick up some tremendous bargains at the very first and second week of April. We had a fantastic year based upon the HCM-BuyLine® catching the turns of reducing exposure to bad market and then catching some bargains when the market turned upwards.

Michael Watkins – Would you speak to how a company like Howard Capital Management and your HCM-BuyLine® technology can help?

Vance Howard – *That's a great question Michael because in the SDBA account, they could use a blend of our three different proprietary mutual funds. The HCM-BuyLine® is overlaid on all of those investments. If they are investing in an HCM SDBA, we do all the heavy lifting on their behalf.*

In other words, when the HCM-BuyLine® triggers, you'll see a third of the money in that fund go to cash, another third if it falls further, etc, as well as when the HCM-BuyLine® turns positive. We aim to remove the stress of watching the market. Investors know they have professionals doing it on their behalf. They know they have math behind the decisions that are being made, not a group of people guessing. And what those five different funds of ours do is it just takes all the work off their shoulders and it gives them a better risk-adjusted outcome. Not only in a pandemic, but also on the upside.

If you look at our returns over the years and our capture of money, we use math to place us in the most productive asset class, whether it's energy, small cap, and biotech, whatever the case may be. By being in a self-directed brokerage window, you can potentially open up thousands of opportunities instead of having only 15 or 20 opportunities inside your 401(k), so you can really aim to maximize your return.

And then again, being a tax deferred account, we can actively trade, and we are not creating a taxable event for the client, so it can be a great opportunity for the individual investor.

Michael Watkins – That's powerful. I just recently learned about the 'Guided Retirement'. Can you explain why you created it and how it works?

Vance Howard – *The 401(k) Optimizer® Guided Retirement is a product of Howard Capital Management. We have a partnership with FIS Relius, one of the largest record-keepers in the world. They house over 150,000 [retirement] plans and over 10 million participants through their software service which can now use 'Guided Retirement.'* Participants gain access to this service by signing up under their company plan, given that company is registered under FIS Relius. For example, let's say Exxon is utilizing FIS Relius. If Exxon were to make an agreement with our offering, the 401(k) Optimizer® Guided Retirement, employees of ExxonMobil with a company-sponsored retirement plan could opt into the 401(k) Optimizer® Guided Retirement and have their account actively managed through the 401(k) Optimizer®. The 401(k) Optimizer® Guided Retirement will automatically rebalance and readjust their portfolio quarterly (if the plan allows), based upon math, to put them in the most productive asset class at any given time, whether that's small-cap, mid-cap, large-cap, international, or whatever the case may be, with a good risk-adjusted portfolio.*

In addition, they will also have access to the <u>HCM-BuyLine</u>® overlay inside their 401(k), so we can automatically reduce exposure to equities in a down market the same way we do everywhere else with the

401(k) Optimizer®. Through this service, we aim to minimize much of the stress and heavy lifting an individual investor has to do, and instead, it'll be done for them. This way they don't have to stay awake at night worrying about the market. They know that they've got math on their side.

Michael Watkins – If the 'Guided Retirement' cannot be installed then plan participants always have a fallback with the 401(k) Optimizer®. Is that correct?

> **Vance Howard** – *That is correct. They can always use the 401(k) Optimizer®. They just need to do everything on their own. It's another pretty large layer of work. What we found, Michael, is that most people, I'd say nine out of ten, they really don't want to spend time doing that. They'd rather sub that out to somebody to manage for them. So, it's really taking a lot of the burden off of them having to do all the heavy lifting themselves.*

Michael Watkins – Right now, millions of Americans have been displaced from their jobs during Covid-19. Also, over a working career, it's not uncommon for people to work for multiple employers and often they are unable to roll their old plans into their new employers' plan. Can you speak to what those orphaned 401(k) plans face when left unattended?

> **Vance Howard** – *I think it's incredibly unwise for any investor to not pay attention to their investments.*

I think what they should do is consolidate all their 401(k)s, potentially roll it into an IRA and engage somebody, such as yourself Michael, to help them, guide them through some turmoil that's clearly happened in the past. And it's clearly going to happen again. So, I think they need to roll them over immediately and have them professionally managed by someone like yourself.

Michael Watkins – Vance, can you give us some insight into the future? Do you see this as a trend, that maybe more plan sponsors will be opening their plans up to the SDBA?

Vance Howard – *I think they absolutely should, Michael. Let me tell you one thing, as a plan sponsor, they have a fiduciary obligation to do what's in the best interest of the client. We were able to witness what happened with the pandemic. What about somebody that didn't have stop-loss risk management like the HCM-BuyLine® on their 401(k)? And let's say the market had not readjusted and improved reasonably, but instead would have been down 50 percent?*

I think there would have been a tremendous number of lawsuits by employees for not at least offering some professional advice to help them navigate such a thing as a pandemics or other shocking things that can happen. So, when you start to look at the offering, I think it's almost a fiduciary obligation that they have to offer things like SDBA.

Michael Watkins – Yeah, which was going to be my next question, Vance. What are the employer's legal responsibilities when sponsoring a plan?

Vance Howard – *Think about this logically. What if the Imperial College would have been correct and we would have had 8, 10, 12, or 15 million American deaths alone from the pandemic and how negatively that could have impacted the market? Evidently, they were way off base – that's not what happened. But think of the liability that each one of those plan sponsors had if they did not offer some sort of active management or professional guidance in such things as a pandemic with stop-loss protection. I think you'd see lawsuits everywhere.*

Michael Watkins – That's a great point Vance and bet you'd be right about all the lawsuits. Now, John Bogle, the founder of The Vanguard Funds, has said openly that he suspects at least two declines of 25-30 percent or maybe even a 50 percent decline is going to happen in the coming decade. https://www.businessinsider.com/jack-bogle-warns-of-two-50-percent-market-declines-in-next-10-years-2013-4

Vance Howard – *But with John Bogle because I've seen that interview too. I like Vanguard Funds. But I am not going to buy and hold anything when their* *founder tells me he's going to lose half my money one of these days. That's just not prudent; be smart.*

Michael Watkins – Right, exactly. Well Vance, this is the end of my questions for you, but is there any additional advice you would like to share with the readers of **The 401(k) Revival?**

Vance Howard – *Well, there are two ways to get experience. You can either live through 10, 20, 30 years of different market turmoil and get experience that way or you can hire an experienced professional. I would suggest that 95 percent of all individual investors should hire out their money management to a proven formula, a proven team that can really make a big impact on their long-term savings and their long-term strategies in their 401(k).*

Michael Watkins – Vance, I appreciate you taking some time out of your busy schedule today so our readers could hear directly from the 401(k) Management Trailblazer himself. Thank you, sir!

Vance Howard – *You're welcome Michael, it was my pleasure.*

CHAPTER 5

Don't Struggle with It

Life is like a combination lock,
your job is to find the right numbers, in the right order,
so you can have anything you want.

– Brian Tracy

As of this writing, the stock market is at its highest levels in history and most 401(k) accounts have recently hit their highest levels ever as well. Exercising caution and prudent money management is perhaps more important to your retirement assets than ever before.

Warren Buffet's Rules for investing.
Rule: #1 Never Lose Money **Rule: #2** See Rule #1

Albert Einstein called compound interest
"The Eighth Wonder of the World". The key to compounding your 401(k) contributions is by having the ability to sidestep the worst Stock Market downturns so compounding can continue uninterrupted.

One main point to understand is when you suffer severe losses you are put into a position of "Catch-up". Think about going backwards with your life savings and losing valuable compounding opportunities to grow wealth. That's pretty terrifying isn't it?

Losses are the greatest negative force working against any wealth building strategy attached to the stock market. Your 401(k) is driven by stock market returns and when it is not monitored daily, it can suffer significant stock market losses. There are new tools available today that can help minimize your losses and maximize your gains. No longer do you have to sit by passively and hope and pray for the stock market to always go up because it doesn't and everyone knows it.

All plan sponsors shoulder a large legal and fiduciary responsibility to inform and educate their employees about the investments inside employer sponsored plans. Many employers do a good job of providing the training and resources their employees need to properly manage their retirement accounts. These employers want to protect their employees from the same financial Armageddon investors suffered during 2000 through 2009 aptly noted as "The Lost Decade"

A traditional 401(k) plan is set up to grow your savings through employee contributions, employer matches, and stock market returns over many years. When properly managed, your 401(k) plan and other investment accounts can experience minimal negative disruption which allows the magic of compounding to happen.

Yes, returns matter; however, risk management should never be overlooked. In fact I would say risk management is equally as important as returns. What's here today could be gone tomorrow and when it's gone, the road back up gets steeper and steeper to climb. It takes a lot longer to claw your way back to where you once were after severe market crashes.

Trying to manage something as complex and ever changing as the investments inside your 401(k) account is very difficult for most people to do successfully. You can spend hundreds of hours researching the perfect basket of mutual funds with the perfect ratios and measure all the statistical data, but when the market crashes, it crashes. The point is you can do all the research and analysis you want, but unless you have a proven *Stop-Loss* strategy in place, the best designed mutual fund itself is helpless to a market crash. (Example: 2000/2008 Market Crashes). There needs be some kind of external warning mechanism or active money manager at the wheel to minimize losses by making the necessary adjustments in a quick and efficient manner.

When I review the performance inside of my clients 401(k)'s, I always seem to get the same *Slack Jawed Response.* Many people are stunned and even angry that this type of savings vehicle was not better designed to protect them from the type of staggering losses they suffered at the turn of the century. Consumers all agree on the same thing: they want to earn more and lose less of their retirement savings. Finding the right balance of offense and defense for your 401(k) can reduce a lot of stress and emotion for you. Don't struggle with it.

Financial Engines & AON Hewitt: In a 2014 Financial Engines/AON Hewitt study, the annual median performance gap return between participants that had help and participants that did not have help was 3.32%, net of fees over the period 2006-2012. This difference can have a meaningful impact on wealth accumulation over time. For a 45-year old participant who seeks the help of a financial professional, it could translate to 79% more wealth at age 65.3 years. Proportionally that translates into an account of $500k growing to $895k under the watchful eyes of a professional money manager. That could mean more fun and more financial security in retirement. Your ending balance will be determined by how you manage your account today.

CHAPTER 6

Orphaned 401 (k) Plans

"Success doesn't come to you. You go to it."

– Marva Collins

Millions of Americans experience job changes during their working career. When leaving an employer, you may also be leaving a 401(k) account behind as well. Some plans will accept new monies from old employer plans and some will not. As soon as you find out a new employer's plan does not accept money from your old employers plan, you should take immediate action to properly house those monies. Remember, these funds belong to you and when you become separated from the old employer, you have full authority to reposition these monies with the money manager of your choice.

According to a January 2018 report from the Bureau of Labor Statistics, the average person changes jobs 10-15 times with an average of 12 job changes over a lifetime. If that is the case some folks could easily own multiple orphaned 401(k) accounts and most likely each one of them is sitting idly without any oversight or **Stop-Loss** protection.

In the event of another market crash, not only could an orphaned 401(k) plan lose a lot of money, but it could also cost the account owner valuable time. Lost opportunity cost is one of the biggest enemies of wealth building. During the 2000-03 and 2008 crashes, it took a combined total of 12 years for the markets to fully recover those losses.

Orphaned 401(k) plans are exposed to many eroding forces like internal fees and downside market volatility. When an old 401(k) plan is left unattended, it must rely solely on positive market gains to stay ahead of inflation measured at 3.22% and internal fees—2.22% national average according to SmartAsset.com. This means you need to get at least 5.45% in gains every year to outpace inflation. The famous investor Warren Buffet calls Inflation *"A Cruel Tax"* and he points out a very important fact of life we should all be keenly aware of. *"Failing to plan is planning to fail."*

Because risk management is a very important element of any wealth building strategy, it's vitally important for any orphaned 401(k) account to be properly repositioned as soon as possible. Many people don't realize how easy it is to rescue a left behind 401(k) account. I help people do this all the time and in most cases, it's just a matter of a quick phone call and setting up the new account paperwork for the funds to transfer.

The best plan of action for reviving an abandoned or orphaned 401(k) account is to have it managed by a professional money manager who pays special attention to risk management. These management firms have the ability to react swiftly in times of a stock market collapse to sidestep the large majority of downside losses. We all witnessed how swift and dramatic the downward spiral was in March of 2020 during the Covid-19 pandemic. In addition to keeping your 401(k) monies in a less volatile environment, you will most likely pay less in fees under the watchful eye of an active money manager compared to all the internal expenses of a 401(k) account.

Every day that goes by, you are one day closer to retirement. Every day you lose money puts you farther behind where you once were and time becomes your enemy. Fees are being charged to your account every day which further erodes your ending balance so it is critically important to always stay on the right side of the market or the erosion to your account could be magnified many times over. Every day your abandoned account drifts without oversight and *Stop-Loss* protection, the closer you could be to a potential financial disaster if another stock market crash or multiple crashes were to happen.

Not paying attention to these orphaned accounts today could cause you severe financial consequences later on. Rescuing a left behind account today could very well provide that extra income needed to splurge in your retirement years. Most folks want to splurge during their retirement years and with health care cost rising at alarming rates and the fears of much higher taxes and inflation creeping in, it's going to be more difficult for future generations to save enough to splurge.

The power of compounding can work wonders for you when you create the proper environment for that to happen. And the opposite can be said when volatile and risky environments are created. Your assets become sitting ducks without a downside defense strategy in place, so be proactive and rescue any left behind 401(k) accounts.

Good financial health is a bit like good physical health. Forming good habits and paying close attention to detail need to happen in order for you to see positive results. The best news about forming good financial health habits for your 401(k) is that you don't have to sweat it. You can leave all the heavy lifting and hard work up to someone else. It's the same equivalent of paying for a gym membership; never showing up to work out, but you still got those amazing results anyway.

So grab the chips and a snack cake. No just kidding. But you get the point. It makes sense to let the professionals who are good at what they do get you the results you are looking for. We are all busy with family and work obligations and it is hard to find the time to do much of anything else. How would it feel knowing your 401(k) financial affairs were being handled by very skilled professionals every minute during stock market trading hours? The confidence and peace of mind knowing you have professional help is priceless.

CHAPTER 7

Solo 401 (k) Plans

"The greater danger for most of us is not that our aim is too high and we miss it, but rather it is too low and we reach it"

– Michelangelo

Owning a small business is no walk in the park and thankfully many tax laws are friendly towards us. The ambitious hard working individuals who dare to blaze a trail for themselves are the heart and soul of the American economy. I love working with these men and women and it has been my distinct honor to work with so many of them.

The solo 401(k) has some distinct advantages over the plan participant 401(k) plans and rightfully so. Solo 401(k)'s are available only to self-employed workers with no employees with an exception for business owners who employ their spouses. Your spouse is the singular exception to the No-Employees rule. As long as they are a part- or full-time employee of the business or co-owner, they can also contribute to your solo 401(k) using income they earned from your business.

To open one of these accounts, you must have an employer identification number (EIN), which you can get from the IRS. You can apply for one of these on the IRS website if your principal business is based in the United States or its territories. The solo is a great option for sole proprietors who want to be able to set aside more money for retirement than an IRA would allow. There are a few extra steps you must take to open a solo account, but it's definitely worth it especially for those who are earning a lot more from their businesses than they are spending right now.

Highlights of the Solo 401(k) plan.

✓ A Solo 401k is perfect for sole proprietors, small businesses, and independent contractors and consultants. Any business with no employees can adopt a Solo 401k plan. The business can be a sole proprietorship, LLC, corporation, or partnership. A Solo 401k plan offers the same advantages as a Self-Directed IRA LLC, but without the need of a custodian. You also do not have to establish an LLC (Limited Liability Company).

✓ Contributions to the plan are completely discretionary. You always have the option to try to contribute as much as legally possible, but you always have the option of reducing or even suspending plan contributions if necessary. In other words, you have the ability to make contributions to your Solo 401k Plan (up to an aggregate amount of $56,000 if you are under the age of 50), but are not required to do so.

✓ With IRAs, those who earn high incomes cannot contribute to a Roth IRA or convert their IRA to a Roth IRA. However, the Solo 401k plan contains a built-in Roth sub- account which can be contributed to without any income restrictions. With a Roth Solo 401k sub-account, you can make Roth type contributions while having the ability to make significantly greater contributions than with an IRA. With the potential of higher tax rates in the future I believe tax sheltered options should be given serious consideration while structuring your post working years income.

✓ A Solo 401k plan can accept rollovers of funds from another retirement savings vehicle, such as an IRA, a SEP, or a previous employer's 401(k) plan. Thus, you can directly rollover your IRA or qualified plan funds to your new 401(k) Plan for investment or loan purposes. Only Roth IRA funds cannot be rolled into a Solo 401k Plan. So for those people wanting to start their own business they have the flexibility to roll their existing 401(k) accounts into a Solo-K.

✓ The Solo 401k plan is unique and popular because it's designed for small, owner-only business. It's a tax-efficient and cost-effective plan that offers all the benefits of a Self- Directed IRA plan, and includes additional benefits. There are many features of the Solo 401(k) Plan that make it so appealing and popular among self-employed business owner.

✓ An IRA only allows a $6,000 contribution limit, with a $1,000 additional "catch up" contribution for those over age 50. However, the Solo 401k annual contribution limit is $57,500 for 2021. There's an additional $6,500 catch-up contribution for those over 50. In addition, your spouse can make high contributions to the plan if he/she generates compensation from the business.

✓ Under the 2021 Solo 401k contribution rules, a plan participant under the age of 50 can make a maximum employee deferral contribution in the amount of $19,500. Make this amount in pre-tax or after-tax (Roth). Then, on the profit sharing side, the business can make 25% contribution up to a combined maximum. This includes the employer deferral of $58,000. For a sole proprietorship or single member LLC, the contribution is 20%.

✓ For plan participants over 50, you can make a maximum employee deferral contribution in the amount of $26,000. Again, you can make this amount in pre-tax or after-tax (Roth). The business can make a 25% profit sharing contribution up to a combined maximum. This includes the employer deferral of $64,500. For sole proprietorships or a single member LLC, the contribution is 20%.

Jason Grantz is a Senior Retirement Director with American Trust Retirement (ATR), a record keeper, service provider custodian at ERISA specialty firm. ATR helps clients with plan set up and other behind the scenes heavy lifting so you, the small business owner, can stay focused on your one thing—your business!

Michael Watkins: Jason, thanks for taking some time for us today.

Jason Grantz: *Absolutely Michael. Glad to help.*

Michael Watkins: So Jason, I list in the book some benefits small business owners canrealize by using a Solo 401(k) plan. Your company ATR is a provider of these and other traditional plans, so I would like you to speak to how these plans actually look to a business professional or consultant.

Jason Grantz: *Basically, you have your owner only, you have your owner plus spouse which is also technically a Solo-K, and because of the family aggregation rules you've got your owner plus spouse plus children too. For example, you can have a dental practice where you have a dentist and a spouse, and the next dentist coming up is the child and that's the only employees of the company, that's technically a Solo 401(k). In this example, everyone is a key employee and everyone is a highly compensated employee; consequently you don't have non-discrimination testing issues like the ones you run into with traditional 401(k) plans.*

Michael Watkins: Solo K's are more flexible than SEP's so let's talk about that for a secondJason?

Jason Grantz: *Prior to the existence of the Solo-K structure, the primary form of owner-only related retirement benefit was a SEP. For a lack of a better* *explanation, these are muscled up IRAs. One advantage that the Solo-K has over a SEP is SEP's have income percentage caps of 25% of gross income capping out at $58k (in 2021). The same hard dollar cap exists in a Solo-K, but you don't have that 25% of income limitation. So, if somebody makes $150k, they could put $58k or $64,500 if they're over 50 in a Solo-K, whereas they would be capped at $37,500k in a SEP.*

Michael Watkins: Business owners like tax friendly structures—can you talk about that aspect of the Solo-K?

Jason Grantz: *With the Solo-K, you've got the ability to choose different tax strategies with the contributions. They can have their employee contributions go in as a Roth, which is an after-tax contribution that grows tax free, and then their profit sharing contribution goes in pre-tax and that contribution will grow tax deferred. So, it allows for the client to diversify their tax strategy with their contributions. Depending on the individual's income, this may be their only opportunity to make a Roth contribution.*

I would like to point out another nice thing about the owner only or owner plus spouse environments. Let's say you have consistently high income earners of $300k to $500k annualized revenue or more. The Solo-K can be paired with a cash balance pension plan for that *same owner and, depending on their age, you can get well north of $100k of tax deferred, tax advantaged dollars saved for that owner and owner spouse.*

Also, someone who is over 50 years old you could get well north of $200k in there and if you can do that for say 10 years straight you'll have a couple million dollars saved for retirement all with tax advantaged dollars. That's going to be very attractive for your entrepreneur who is running a sole proprietorship or owner only corporation.

When talking to that person's accountant about strategies to maximize their tax advantaged savings and strategies to minimize their current tax paid as well as strategies to delay the time for when they do have to pay taxes, these strategies can be incredibly attractive. Of course, we at American Trust provide all of these types of plans and services.

Michael Watkins: Jason I appreciate your contribution to this book.

Jason Grantz: *It's truly been my pleasure and thank you very much for including me.*

CHAPTER 8

Less Equals "MORE"

The Best Things in Life Are Tax Free.

– Joseph Bonkowski

"Numbers don't lie; people do" is an old saying. When you sign up for a 401(k) plan you agree to take a tax deduction up front and defer paying any taxes until you make withdrawals. By agreeing to pay taxes many years into the future at an unknown future tax rate, it becomes very hard to know what the after tax net return will be. Your 401(k) business partner is "Uncle Sam" and he enforces tax rates the United States Congress passes into law which are subject to change quickly and without warning.

"The Rich Just Keep Getting Richer" is another old saying. That is true on some levels; however, just because you have a lot of money doesn't mean by default you will continue to grow that wealth. You need to work hard at growing your wealth and become "Tax Savvy" if you want to outpace inflation and severe taxation. Tax reduction is a major component to any wealth building strategy. With the

proper tax guidance and leadership, average Americans have the opportunity to live a much less stressful retirement life by having more non-taxable money to spend.

Our elected officials in Washington D.C. have spent enormous amounts of money over the last 20 years. They have put this nation 28 trillion dollars in debt which will at some point have very real consequences. I think you can guess what those consequences might be so beware to all.

> "America is a land of taxation that was founded to avoid taxation." **Laurence J. Peter**

My next contributor to The 401(k) Revival has some raw data to share with you that is very compelling. It's not about how much money you make it's more about how much money you get to keep. And if you think tax rates may be higher or significantly higher in the future, I believe you will find this chapter very interesting.

Tom Mishoe is an Investment Advisor Representative with Horter Investment Management and a Certified Public Accountant. Tom primarily works with business owners and professionals by showing them how the targeted use of our tax savings strategies contained in the tax codes enable them to save, in many cases, hundreds of thousands of dollars over time. In this chapter, Tom will break down the tax strategy of pay now or pay later.

Key Definitions

The definitions provided below are excerpts from www.Investopedia.com.

Qualified Retirement Plans

Qualified retirement plans are designed to meet ERISA *(Employee Retirement Income Security Act of 1974)* guidelines and, as such, *qualify for tax benefits* on top of those received by regular retirement plans, such as IRAs. In some cases, employers deduct an allowable portion of pretax dollars from the employee's wages for investment in the qualified plan. *The contributions and earnings then grow tax deferred until withdrawal.*

A qualified plan may have either a defined-contribution or defined-benefit structure. In a defined-contribution plan, employees select investments, and the retirement amount will depend on the decisions they made. With a defined-benefit plan, there is a guaranteed payout amount and the risk of investing is borne by the employer.

Plan sponsors must meet a number of guidelines regarding participation, vesting, and benefit accrual, funding and plan information to qualify their plans under ERISA.

Non-Qualified Retirement Plans

Many employers offer primary employee's non-qualified retirement plans as part of a benefits or executive package. *Non-qualified plans are those that are not eligible for tax-deferred benefits under ERISA. Consequently, deducted contributions for nonqualified plans are taxed when the income is recognized. In other words, the employee will pay taxes on the funds before they are contributed to the plan.*

Qualified vs Non-Qualified

The main difference between the two plans is the tax treatment of deductions by employers, but there are also other differences. Qualified plans have tax-deferred contributions from the employee, and employers may deduct amounts they contribute to the plan. Nonqualified plans use after-tax dollars to fund them, and in most cases employers cannot claim their contributions as a tax deduction.

Why Consider Taxes When Selecting An Approach To Retirement Investing?

The short story.

There is a place for both Qualified and Non-Qualified investments for most people investing in their retirement future. But there is an important trade-off relating to taxes that must be considered and addressed at the initial time of investment but also at various points thereafter.

Think of it in this way.

If you were a farmer, would you prefer to be taxed on the **SEED** you plant or would you rather be taxed on the **HARVEST** you reap? You WILL be taxed on your retirement account, either when you contribute your money to your retirement account or when you withdraw the money from your retirement account. The selection of how you opt to be taxed on your retirement accounts can have a **huge impact** on the ultimate value of an investment portfolio identified for retirement income. Let's take a simple example to show the impact of taxes on a retirement portfolio.

Assumptions:

Income: $120,000 per year

Investment Amount: $12,000 per year (on first day of the year)

Effective Tax Rate: 35%

Investment Earnings Rate: 8%

Withdrawals: $30,000 net after taxes (on first day of the year)

Note: While the effective tax rates and investment earnings rates will likely vary (maybe substantially) from the time of investment until the time of withdrawal, keeping these rates consistent will simplify the illustration of the results of the tax strategy utilized.

Compare the summary results of these two separate investments:

	Qualified Investment	Non-Qualified Investment
Investments, net of tax	$360,000	$234,000
Accumulated investment balance	$1,468,150	$954,298
Withdrawals (30 years), net of tax	$900,000	$900,000
Remaining balance	$247,141	$160,642
Total withdrawals	$1,147,141	$1,060,642
Tax paid (saved) before investment	($126,000)	$126,000
Tax paid on withdrawals over 30 years	$484,615	$0
Tax paid on remaining balance	$89,499	$0
Total Tax Paid	$448,114	$126,000
Total Withdrawals, Net Of Tax	$699,027	$934,642

Non-Qualified Investment Accumulation Analysis

Period	Salary	Retirement Investment At 10%	Tax Paid (Saved) At 35%	Net Retirement Investment	Earnings At 8%	Accumulated Retirement Investment
1	$120,000	$12,000	$4,200	$7,800	$624	$8,424
2	$120,000	$12,000	$4,200	$7,800	$1,297.92	$17,521.92
3	$120,000	$12,000	$4,200	$7,800	$2,025.75	$27,347.67
4	$120,000	$12,000	$4,200	$7,800	$2,811.81	$37,959.49

5	$120,000	$12,000	$4,200	$7,800	$3,660.76	$49,420.25
6	$120,000	$12,000	$4,200	$7,800	$4,577.62	$61,797.87
7	$120,000	$12,000	$4,200	$7,800	$5,567.83	$75,165.70
8	$120,000	$12,000	$4,200	$7,800	$6,637.26	$89,602.95
9	$120,000	$12,000	$4,200	$7,800	$7,792.24	$105,195.19
10	$120,000	$12,000	$4,200	$7,800	$9,039.61	$122,034.80
11	$120,000	$12,000	$4,200	$7,800	$10,386.78	$140,221.59
12	$120,000	$12,000	$4,200	$7,800	$11,841.73	$159,863.31
13	$120,000	$12,000	$4,200	$7,800	$13,413.07	$181,076.38
14	$120,000	$12,000	$4,200	$7,800	$15,110.11	$203,986.49
15	$120,000	$12,000	$4,200	$7,800	$16,942.92	$228,729.41
16	$120,000	$12,000	$4,200	$7,800	$18,922.35	$255,451.76
17	$120,000	$12,000	$4,200	$7,800	$21,060.14	$284,311.90
18	$120,000	$12,000	$4,200	$7,800	$23,368.95	$315,480.85
19	$120,000	$12,000	$4,200	$7,800	$25,862.47	$349,143.32
20	$120,000	$12,000	$4,200	$7,800	$28,555.47	$385,498.79
21	$120,000	$12,000	$4,200	$7,800	$31,463.90	$424,762.69
22	$120,000	$12,000	$4,200	$7,800	$34,605.02	$467,167.71
23	$120,000	$12,000	$4,200	$7,800	$37,997.42	$512,965.12
24	$120,000	$12,000	$4,200	$7,800	$41,661.21	$562,426.33
25	$120,000	$12,000	$4,200	$7,800	$45,618.11	$615,844.44
26	$120,000	$12,000	$4,200	$7,800	$49,891.56	$673,535.99
27	$120,000	$12,000	$4,200	$7,800	$54,506.88	$735,842.87
28	$120,000	$12,000	$4,200	$7,800	$59,491.43	$803,134.30
29	$120,000	$12,000	$4,200	$7,800	$64,874.74	$875,809.05
30	$120,000	$12,000	$4,200	$7,800	$70,688.72	$954,297.77
Total		$360,000	$126,000	$234,000	$720,297.77	

Assumptions:

Income: $120,000 per year

Investment Amount: $12,000 per year (on first day of period)

Effective Tax Rate: 35%

Investment Earnings Rate: 8%

Withdrawals: $30,000 net after taxes (on first day of period)

Note: While the effective tax rates and investment earnings rates will likely vary (maybe substantially) from the time of investment until the time of withdrawal, keeping these rates consistent will simplify the illustration of the results of the tax strategy utilized.

Non-Qualified Investment Distribution Analysis

Period	Retirement Investment Balance	Withdrawal	Earnings At 8%	Tax Paid (Saved) At 35%
31	$954,297.77	$30,000.00	$76,343.82	$0.00
32	$1,000,641.59	$30,000.00	$77,651.33	$0.00
33	$970,641.59	$30,000.00	$75,251.33	$0.00
34	$940,641.59	$30,000.00	$72,851.33	$0.00
35	$910,641.59	$30,000.00	$70,451.33	$0.00
36	$880,641.59	$30,000.00	$68,051.33	$0.00
37	$850,641.59	$30,000.00	$65,651.33	$0.00
38	$820,641.59	$30,000.00	$63,251.33	$0.00

39	$790,641.59	$30,000.00	$60,851.33	$0.00
40	$760,641.59	$30,000.00	$58,451.33	$0.00
41	$730,641.59	$30,000.00	$56,051.33	$0.00
42	$700,641.59	$30,000.00	$53,651.33	$0.00
43	$670,641.59	$30,000.00	$51,251.33	$0.00
44	$640,641.59	$30,000.00	$48,851.33	$0.00
45	$610,641.59	$30,000.00	$46,451.33	$0.00
46	$580,641.59	$30,000.00	$44,051.33	$0.00
47	$550,641.59	$30,000.00	$41,651.33	$0.00
48	$520,641.59	$30,000.00	$39,251.33	$0.00
49	$490,641.59	$30,000.00	$36,851.33	$0.00
50	$460,641.59	$30,000.00	$34,451.33	$0.00
51	$430,641.59	$30,000.00	$32,051.33	$0.00
52	$400,641.59	$30,000.00	$29,651.33	$0.00
53	$370,641.59	$30,000.00	$27,251.33	$0.00
54	$340,641.59	$30,000.00	$24,851.33	$0.00
55	$310,641.59	$30,000.00	$22,451.33	$0.00
56	$280,641.59	$30,000.00	$20,051.33	$0.00
57	$250,641.59	$30,000.00	$17,651.33	$0.00
58	$220,641.59	$30,000.00	$15,251.33	$0.00
59	$190,641.59	$30,000.00	$12,851.33	$0.00
60	$160,641.59	$30,000.00	$10,451.33	$0.00
Total		$900,000.00		$0.00

Assumptions:

Income: $120,000 per year

Investment Amount: $12,000 per year (on first day of period)

Effective Tax Rate: 35%

Investment Earnings Rate: 8%

Withdrawals: $30,000 net after taxes (on first day of period)

Note: While the effective tax rates and investment earnings rates will likely vary (maybe substantially) from the time of investment until the time of withdrawal, keeping these rates consistent will simplify the illustration of the results of the tax strategy utilized.

Qualified Investment Accumulation Analysis

$120,000	$12,000	($4,200)	$12,000	$1,996.80	$26,956.80
$120,000	$12,000	($4,200)	$12,000	$3,116.54	$42,073.34
$120,000	$12,000	($4,200)	$12,000	$4,325.87	$58,399.21
$120,000	$12,000	($4,200)	$12,000	$5,631.94	$76,031.15
$120,000	$12,000	($4,200)	$12,000	$7,042.49	$95,073.64
$120,000	$12,000	($4,200)	$12,000	$8,565.89	$115,639.53
$120,000	$12,000	($4,200)	$12,000	$10,211.16	$137,850.69
$120,000	$12,000	($4,200)	$12,000	$11,988.06	$161,838.75
$120,000	$12,000	($4,200)	$12,000	$13,907.10	$187,745.85

$120,000	$12,000	($4,200)	$12,000	$15,979.67	$215,725.52
$120,000	$12,000	($4,200)	$12,000	$18,218.04	$245,943.56
$120,000	$12,000	($4,200)	$12,000	$20,635.48	$278,579.04
$120,000	$12,000	($4,200)	$12,000	$23,246.32	$313,825.37
$120,000	$12,000	($4,200)	$12,000	$26,066.03	$351,891.40
$120,000	$12,000	($4,200)	$12,000	$29,111.31	$393,002.71
$120,000	$12,000	($4,200)	$12,000	$32,400.22	$437,402.92
$120,000	$12,000	($4,200)	$12,000	$35,952.23	$485,355.16
$120,000	$12,000	($4,200)	$12,000	$39,788.41	$537,143.57
$120,000	$12,000	($4,200)	$12,000	$43,931.49	$593,075.06
$120,000	$12,000	($4,200)	$12,000	$48,406.00	$653,481.06
$120,000	$12,000	($4,200)	$12,000	$53,238.48	$718,719.55
$120,000	$12,000	($4,200)	$12,000	$58,457.56	$789,177.11
$120,000	$12,000	($4,200)	$12,000	$64,094.17	$865,271.28
$120,000	$12,000	($4,200)	$12,000	$70,181.70	$947,452.98
$120,000	$12,000	($4,200)	$12,000	$76,756.24	$1,036,209.22
$120,000	$12,000	($4,200)	$12,000	$83,856.74	$1,132,065.96
$120,000	$12,000	($4,200)	$12,000	$91,525.28	$1,235,591.23
$120,000	$12,000	($4,200)	$12,000	$99,807.30	$1,347,398.53
$120,000	$12,000	($4,200)	$12,000	$108,751.88	$1,468,150.42
	$360,000	**($126,000)**	**$360,000**	**$1,108,150.42**	

Assumptions:

Income: $120,000 per year

Investment Amount: $12,000 per year (on first day of period)

Effective Tax Rate: 35%

Investment Earnings Rate: 8%

Withdrawals: $30,000 net after taxes (on first day of period)

Note: While the effective tax rates and investment earnings rates will likely vary (maybe substantially) from the time of investment until the time of withdrawal, keeping these rates consistent will simplify the illustration of the results of the tax strategy utilized.

Qualified Investment Distribution Analysis

Period	Retirement Investment Balance	Withdrawal	Earnings At 8%	Tax Paid (Saved) At 35%	Net Withdrawal
31	$1,468,150.42	$46,153.85	$117,452.03	$16,153.85	$30,000.00
32	$1,539,448.60	$46,153.85	$119,463.58	$16,153.85	$30,000.00
33	$1,493,294.75	$46,153.85	$115,771.27	$16,153.85	$30,000.00
34	$1,447,140.90	$46,153.85	$112,078.96	$16,153.85	$30,000.00
35	$1,400,987.05	$46,153.85	$108,386.66	$16,153.85	$30,000.00
36	$1,354,833.20	$46,153.85	$104,694.35	$16,153.85	$30,000.00
37	$1,308,679.35	$46,153.85	$101,002.04	$16,153.85	$30,000.00
38	$1,262,525.50	$46,153.85	$97,309.73	$16,153.85	$30,000.00
39	$1,216,371.65	$46,153.85	$93,617.42	$16,153.85	$30,000.00
40	$1,170,217.80	$46,153.85	$89,925.12	$16,153.85	$30,000.00
41	$1,124,063.95	$46,153.85	$86,232.81	$16,153.85	$30,000.00

42	$1,077,910.10	$46,153.85	$82,540.50	$16,153.85	$30,000.00
43	$1,031,756.25	$46,153.85	$78,848.19	$16,153.85	$30,000.00
44	$985,602.40	$46,153.85	$75,155.88	$16,153.85	$30,000.00
45	$939,448.55	$46,153.85	$71,463.58	$16,153.85	$30,000.00
46	$893,294.70	$46,153.85	$67,771.27	$16,153.85	$30,000.00
47	$847,140.85	$46,153.85	$64,078.96	$16,153.85	$30,000.00
48	$800,987.00	$46,153.85	$60,386.65	$16,153.85	$30,000.00
49	$754,833.15	$46,153.85	$56,694.34	$16,153.85	$30,000.00
50	$708,679.30	$46,153.85	$53,002.04	$16,153.85	$30,000.00
51	$662,525.45	$46,153.85	$49,309.73	$16,153.85	$30,000.00
52	$616,371.60	$46,153.85	$45,617.42	$16,153.85	$30,000.00
53	$570,217.75	$46,153.85	$41,925.11	$16,153.85	$30,000.00
54	$524,063.90	$46,153.85	$38,232.80	$16,153.85	$30,000.00
55	$477,910.05	$46,153.85	$34,540.50	$16,153.85	$30,000.00
56	$431,756.20	$46,153.85	$30,848.19	$16,153.85	$30,000.00
57	$385,602.35	$46,153.85	$27,155.88	$16,153.85	$30,000.00
58	$339,448.50	$46,153.85	$23,463.57	$16,153.85	$30,000.00
59	$293,294.65	$46,153.85	$19,771.26	$16,153.85	$30,000.00
60	$247,140.80	$46,153.85	$16,078.96	$16,153.85	$30,000.00
		$1,384,615.50	$2,082,818.80	$484,615.43	$900,000.07

Assumptions:

Income: $120,000 per year

Investment Amount: $12,000 per year (on first day of period)

Effective Tax Rate: 35%

Investment Earnings Rate: 8%

Withdrawals: $30,000 net after taxes (on first day of period)

Note: While the effective tax rates and investment earnings rates will likely vary (maybe substantially) from the time of investment until the time of withdrawal, keeping these rates consistent will simplify the illustration of the results of the tax strategy utilized.

Note that even though the investments into the Non-Qualified Investment account are significantly less, resulting in a significantly lower accumulated balance, the non-taxable nature of the withdrawals result in no distribution taxes, significantly less taxes over the lifetime of the investment and significantly more distributions, net of taxes.

Many investors believe that a qualified account will produce better results due to their belief that the tax rates, which will be applied to their retirement withdrawals, will be significantly lower than the rates applied when they make their investments, thus producing positive "tax arbitrage". While future tax rates are unknown, one must ask themselves whether they believe that future tax rates being applied to their withdrawals will be significantly lower than today's tax rates.

> "What the government gives it must first take away"
> **John S. Coleman**

Of course, the analysis of the appropriate retirement plan contribution approach and amount of contributions may vary by investor and may vary by time. A young investor may find they cannot pay taxes and contribute to a non-qualified plan at a level comparable to contribution in a qualified plan with an immediate tax deduction. This requires the assistance of a financial planner who fully understands these concepts and can help the investor understand the ramifications of their choices. The financial planner may also help the investor maximize their retirement plan contributions, whether into a qualified or non-qualified plan. And, of course, this management of retirement contributions should be an "ongoing process rather than an event." Individual circumstances, and contribution abilities, can change over time. And many investors change their minds.

It is not unusual to see investors initially invest in a qualified plan and utilize the immediate tax deduction but later determine that they would rather pay taxes on a smaller accumulated amount and transfer their qualified money into a non-qualified plan (i.e., Roth IRA). While this conversion approach may not reduce total taxes as much as the example above, the conversion may save significant taxes over a lifetime.

As an investor, it's important to find a knowledgeable financial planner and/or other professional that specializes in tax planning. They can help you understand and appropriately implement these tax savings strategies.

When you think about it realistically the big bad government is actually not so bad because they have given all of us workarounds to paying certain types and levels of taxes. What they so accurately assume is that a very small percentage of people will ever look for those tax solutions. This is very true and another reason why the rich keep getting richer. Simply put the rich have surrounded themselves with tax saving professionals to guide them through the maze of tax law.

> "What you don't know you don't know... and sometimes what you think you know really isn't so." **Jim Rohn**

CHAPTER 9

401 (k) Investing Made Easy

Planning is bringing the future into the present,
so that you can do something about it

— Alan Lakein

In this chapter, you will get a better understanding of how far 401(k) management has come in recent years. Howard Capital Management has been the trailblazer in this space and I appreciate Vance Howard and his team for participating in this project and sharing their sage advice with all of us. 401(k) investors all over America are starting to see the meaningful difference professional management can have on their 401(k) ending balances. This is a trend that could see the next wave of 401(k) investors saving significantly more for their retirements than their baby boomer parents did.

Some companies go out of their way to ensure their employees are given top notch advice and leadership in this area. Why? Well, the employer, as the plan sponsor, is overseen by regulatory bodies and has a high level of legal and fiduciary responsibility to provide their employees professional guidance.

The 401(k) world is often times a very complex space to venture into and employers need to navigate these waters very carefully. Building the right team around themselves in the beginning is critical for the plan's health and the employee's financial wellbeing. It's been my experience that most employers truly want to help their employees improve their financial future and they do the best they can when dealing with such a complex monstrosity like the 401(k) plan.

My goal is to help the everyday working Americans save significantly more for their retirements than the previous generations were able to do using their employer sponsored 401(k) plan. I also want to help business owners reduce their liability exposure by helping them install the most efficient risk management tools I know. Risk management is key to building significant wealth and avoiding large market losses, and is generally not something most 401(k) plans have the capability of doing.

I believe employee retention and company loyalty will improve when employers create an environment for success unlike any other companies in their market place. After all, when you have the opportunity to potentially save more and lose less inside one's 401(k) account, it can help remove the stressful emotions of trying to manage something as foreign and confusing as a 401(k) plan.

Cole Staton with Howard Capital Management joined me for an interview where he shared how new developments in technology can assist hard working Americans participating in employer sponsored plans. Having access to these tools could greatly decrease one's risk exposure and potentially increase the ability to gain more. I also interviewed Steve Albritton with Howard Capital Management (HCM) to discuss how plan participants can put their 401(k) plan on full autopilot. Steve discusses the 2-R or Self-Directed Brokerage Account (SDBA) option and how to properly set it up and the benefits of professional management.

Michael Watkins: Cole, I want to thank you for joining me today and let's begin with explaining a technology service anyone can use on their own regardless of what options their employer sponsored plan might offer.

> *Cole Staton: Sure, Michael. The 401(k) Optimizer® is a subscription service and online tool created by Howard Capital Management (HCM) over twelve years ago. The system is a computerized tool that evaluates the individual's risk tolerance, goals, and available funds and their key variables in the plan to generate personalized portfolio allocation recommendations. In addition, the 401(k) Optimizer® utilizes HCM's proprietary risk management indicator, the HCM-BuyLine®, to mathematically navigate major market downturns by reducing equity*

*exposure during major downturns and increasing
equity exposure during market upturns. This is a very
unique feature for individuals that can help remove
emotion from the investing process as well as
potentially dramatically affect their long-term gains.
The system is designed to guide them through the
evaluation and implementation process.*

Michael Watkins: Cole, I know HCM has two other professionally managed services for 401(k) participants, but when a plan does not allow for those services to be used, any individual with a company-sponsored retirement plan can use the 401(k) Optimizer® tool, correct?

> **Cole Staton:** *Yes, that is correct. If you have a
> 401(k), 403(B), 457, 401(a) or a Thrift Savings Plan
> (TSP), you have the ability to work with the 401(k)
> Optimizer®, or TSP Optimizer®. As long as the
> individual has a company-sponsored retirement
> plan, they can utilize the 401(k) Optimizer®.*
>
> *Additionally, we believe the 401(k) Optimizer®
> could be a great value and alternative for those who
> do not have the ability to opt into a managed account
> solution or similar active management option inside
> their plan.*

Michael Watkins: Now let's discuss the next level of technology—the managed account solution designed to work with the core investment line up of participants' plans.

Cole Staton: *The 401(k) Optimizer® Guided Retirement is designed to perform a step further by generating and then delivering the personalized recommendations directly to the participant's plan for implementation on their behalf. We essentially connect our managed account solution to a 401(k) plan, so plan participants can access the 401(k) Optimizer® allocation and trade recommendations within their company plan as well as gain access to the HCM-BuyLine® overlay to mitigate downside risk.*

'Guided Retirement' is programmed to quantitatively select investments by analyzing the available funds' expense ratios, Morningstar® rating and performance history to then generate the most efficient portfolio for the individual. The system also rebalances quarterly (if the plan allows) based on current market conditions, keeping in mind their risk profile and return objective. And again, any updated trade recommendations are delivered to the plan provider to be implemented on the participant's behalf.

NOTE: The HCM-BuyLine® is a proprietary algorithm Howard Capital Management uses for their own trading purposes that aims to remove emotional decisions from the investing process.

Michael Watkins: Cole, when you mention reducing equity exposure during major market downturns, what asset classes does the technology typically indicate to move to?

> **Cole Staton:** *Great question. When the HCM-BuyLine® indicates a major sell signal, the system mathematically and quantitatively recommends moving the proposed assets into less risk investment options such as short-term T-bills, intermediate term bonds, cash and/or cash equivalents.*

Michael Watkins: Let's discuss how to implement the 'Guided Retirement' strategy for a plan participant?

> **Cole Staton:** *From a software integration level, 401(k) Optimizer® Guided Retirement is currently available to roughly 150,000 plans. However, it is determined by the plan provider if they would like to integrate the 'Guided Retirement' solution in their plan. If they do agree to utilize 'Guided Retirement,' the service will be available to the participant. The participant will see this option when logging into their 401(k) account to check their balance or select their investment options, and it is at their will to "opt in" to the service.*

Michael Watkins: Cole, let's talk about the benefits a small business owner could enjoy from their employees participating in one of your platforms. Can you speak more on that?

Cole Staton: *'Guided Retirement' is designed to be a seamless integration and could benefit business owners as it comes at no cost to them individually – all the costs associated with this service is going to be borne from participant accounts.*

We see this solution as a great way to invest in an employee's financial health and well-being because employers are giving them access to an experienced money manager with integrated risk management methodology and a historical track record that demonstrates the amount of wealth accrued for clients over that time period.

And two, this can be a great employee retention tool [in my opinion]. Employers are not only investing in their employees' future, but providing an investment option that could help them be competitive in keeping top talent by offering such a benefit. Additionally, employers are potentially reducing the amount of stress and anxiety around investment selection and allocation for their long-term goals.

It's now [April 2021] been over a year since COVID really started to spike in March [2020] and we saw a significant sell off in the stock market. Many investors were scrambling and allowing their emotions to dictate their investing decisions. But on the contrary perspective, Howard Capital Management was not scrambling because we have a repeatable, mathematical, quantitative process in place with the HCM-BuyLine®.

We trusted in the HCM-BuyLine® because math was telling us to reduce equity exposure at certain points in time and we were able to avoid 70-80% of the significant downtrend while capturing 70-80% of that uptrend as we ran out of March and into April. So it's a great way to give people direction when they need it the most, in my opinion.

Michael Watkins: That's amazing Cole. Thanks for sharing.

Cole Staton: *My pleasure Michael.*

Next, Steve Allbritton with Howard Capital Management explains the professional 401(k) management offered through a 401(k) plan's SDBA option. This option opens an entirely new window of investment opportunities for the plan participant. Inside this window, the investor will enjoy many investment options not offered inside their plans core lineup. Steve explains how this option can put your 401(k) on total autopilot.

Michael Watkins: Steve, can you explain exactly what the SDBA option is inside a 401(k) plan?

Steve Allbritton: *Sure, Michael! Company plans that offer a SDBA allow any plan participant the ability to move their assets or a portion of their assets, tax- and penalty-free, into a brokerage account and choose from a larger selection of investment choices. It is important to understand that their assets remain in the retirement plan; they are not rolled over and there is no taxable event. Through Howard Capital Management's tactical, active management strategy, a plan participant can relax knowing their investments are being carefully managed in accordance with their particular risk-tolerance profile.*

Michael Watkins: How does HCM provide 401(k) money management services to 401(k) plan participants?

Steve Allbritton: *After the advisor meets with the plan participant and determines their risk profile, the participant will complete the necessary onboarding paperwork (with the advisor's assistance) that gives Howard Capital Management the authorization to place a trade for one of four HCM Mutual Fund Models in the participant's Self-Directed Brokerage Account (SDBA). And the participant does not have to pay any sort of external management fee via a 'bill'. All fees for the HCM SDBA Models are taken out of the internal expenses of the funds and are already reflected in the daily mutual fund performance figures.*

Michael Watkins: HCM uses a proprietary technology that has saved their clients from major losses as well as made their clients large sums of money over the past 20 plus years. Tell us about how this works?

> *Steve Allbritton: With the twists and turns of the market, human emotions often get in the way of the average investor, deterring the average investor from making rational decisions about their investments, and reaching their investment goals. Missing the worst days of the market could save them much more than they think; it could save them years of catching up. With HCM's fiduciary investment advice through the utilization of the HCM-BuyLine® (Howard Capital Management's proprietary Stop-Loss indicator), HCM can manage a participant's assets in their SDBA account (based upon their risk-tolerance) and will adjust their portfolio on an as-needed basis, thus aiming to remove emotion from the investing process!*

Michael Watkins: There seems to be a big push on fee reduction in today's market place. Would you speak to how the fees for this service get paid?

> *Steve Allbritton: Remember, the client does not receive any sort of "external bill" for the HCM model management in their SDBA. Howard Capital Management is compensated for their services (and for that of the soliciting advisor assisting the participant) through the internal expenses of funds' share class.*

Michael Watkins: What is the biggest benefit clients will realize?

Steve Allbritton: Many plan participants owning Howard Capital Management's SDBA Mutual Fund Models in their 401(k) SDBA enjoy the 'upside' potential of owning high-quality mutual funds, but also rest a little easier knowing their retirement assets are under the 'watchful eye' of the HCM-BuyLine®, which has historically kept HCM investors on the right-side of the market for over two decades.

Michael Watkins: You elaborated on the COVID crash that happened last March/April on my podcast, RetirementTampaBay.com, and I think it's noteworthy for the readers to understand sidestepping market volatility. Would you paint a clear picture of how the HCM-BuyLine® performed during that period of time?

Steve Allbritton: *Sure, Michael! The HCM-BuyLine® first signaled a reduction in risk in the HCM SDBA Fund Models on March 10, 2020. The second "confirming" signal hit on March 12, and even further risk reduction was taken in the Models. On April 14, 2020, the HCM-BuyLine® put out an "all clear" signal and the SDBA Fund Models were fully reinvested. The HCM-BuyLine® is designed to help us avoid large market downturns and also capture a large portion of subsequent market* *upturns. There is a 20 plus year track record people can view on our website at Howardcm.com.*

Michael Watkins: Thanks for sharing how the SDBA option works as well as the HCM-BuyLine® strategy.

Steve Allbritton: My pleasure, Michael.

CHAPTER 10

Change For The Better

"I can't change the direction of the wind, but I can adjust my sails to always reach my destination"

— Jimmy Dean

Change is without question one of the most uncomfortable things for human beings to do successfully. By design, humans have a herd or tribe mentally and sometimes we find ourselves moving in a certain direction simply because everyone around us is. In the investment world, just because a product or service is popular doesn't mean it's the correct or right thing for your financial situation. Change is necessary throughout life and great outcomes are achieved by thoughtful, forward looking, and informed decisions.

Michael Miles famously said, *"The essence of life is change"*. Change is the only constant. It seems surprising that we tend to resist change, but I believe that we should embrace it. It is going to happen to us in one form or another, so why not take control of it and proactively shape ourselves? We are always moving either in the direction of growth or the direction of decay so why not decide to grow and become better than we are?

There are two stories I love to tell regarding change. The first story is taken from the book *Awareness written by Anthony de Mello. An eagle lays an egg but somehow the egg finds its way into a chicken coup. A chicken incubates the egg with all her others and when it hatches, she rears the eagle as if it were one of her own chicks. It learns to peck the dust for food, flap its wings, and strut around the farmyard. One day, an eagle flies by overhead and the little eagle looks up and sees this and says to himself "I wish I were an eagle, how majestic, how free, and how beautiful to be like that and have such a life." The eagle lived like a chicken and died like a chicken because that is what he thought.*

The next story is from Eckhart Tolle's *The Power of Now. There was a beggar sitting on an old wooden box, and he's been sitting there for years. He sits on the street and begs for money. One day, someone walks past and tells the old beggar that he doesn't have anything to give except a piece of information. The stranger tells the old man that his wooden box is full of money and treasure. The old man laughs and soon forgets what the stranger told him. He dies without ever opening the box.*

These stories perfectly sum up this quote by **Jim Rohn.** "You don't know what you don't know, and sometimes what you think you know really isn't so".

There is a great correlation between these two stories and the 401(k) investor. Neither the eagle nor the old beggar had the knowledge or awareness to experience the full potential of their lives. They lived lives of mediocrity because they lacked the desire to learn and explore, so they settled for life as it was. Likewise, today's 401(k) investors are never taught how to fully maximize and harness the amazing power inside their 401(k) plans through the 2-R/SDBA options. The majority of 401(k) investors will never dare to look for anything other than what is set in front of them. They settle for mediocrity and accept whatever comes their way. But not you! By your own curiosity, a gift of knowledge that can transform your financial future for the better is right in front of you. It's as simple as learning how professional help can get you the results you are looking for.

When you consider how we are bombarded with endless advertising every day, it's no wonder so many folks are confused and bewildered regarding their financial dealings. We are being told that this person or that company is the very Best, Most Honest, #1 Rated, etc., and by what metric are they using to come up with those labels? In our daily travels, we see billboards and signs everywhere and if we are listening to the radio, we get hit with more advertising from the air waves.

Advertisers know where we go by our age, buying habits, and geographical location. When we pick up one of our favorite magazines there are a host of ads jumping off the pages at us. Advertisers are targeting us online as well; for example, just type in a search query on the computer or smart phone and almost instantly a flood of ads similar to the one you just searched for appear out of nowhere. That's called retargeting and it is one of the most widely used forms of online advertising in the 21st century.

Advertisers also understand that by sheer repetition, many of us will eventually submit to their call to action if we just see or hear or see it enough times. In this fast paced world we live in, far too often many of us come away from a purchase or service agreement with buyer's remorse. Many times, that is a direct result of not fully understanding the product or service.

I found my greatest success to making positive and lasting changes was to surround myself with professionals who have great knowledge in specific areas. You may have heard the term "Baby Steps." For lasting change to take root, many life coaches and teachers of change management agree that small bite size chunks help to usher in the lasting change you want for your life.

One example is the weight I lost by modifying my diet and walking daily which has also increased my energy level. I also have better mental clarity and a more positive outlook on my life as a result. My inner circle of professionals helped me learn what works best for me. By listening to and implementing their sage advice, I have been able to make positive transformations which have also spilled over into my professional life. So taking a few small "baby steps" today can lead to amazing results in the future.

By taking a small step in managing your investments, you could delegate all the heavy lifting to someone else. How would you feel knowing highly skilled people were monitoring your account and that those professionals could take immediate action to protect your 401(k) account from significant losses during a market crash? How would it feel to view the next stock market crash as the next great wealth building opportunity?

Making the appropriate changes today could bring more peace of mind and confidence to your retirement life tomorrow. Today's financial world can be full of confusion and loud noise, but there is also a place of quiet confidence and peace of mind. Professional money managers can help you by taking all of the emotion out of what some folks consider an overwhelming and very stressful task.

We have all heard the phrase "The rich just keep getting richer." It's not by luck or magic these folks continue to build wealth year over year. They use money managers and tax planners to strategically grow their assets and protect them from major losses and taxation. Building wealth through stock market investments can turn middle class wage earners into wealthy retirees. When highly skilled people are at the wheel guiding and making adjustments in real time, you can rest easy knowing your finances are in very capable hands. By making a few simple changes to your wealth building strategies today, you can produce very meaningful results tomorrow. There may only be a few degrees of separation between your present path and achieving your ideal retirement life. This is a critical point in time that your future life is depending on. You must get it right now because tomorrow may be too late.

CHAPTER 11
It's Always Too Early

"Come to the edge he said. They said, We are afraid.
Come to the edge he said. They came. He pushed them,
And They Flew!

– Guillaume Apollinaire

It's always too early to plan until it's too late is an old saying among Financial Professionals.

The more time you have to compound your savings, the better your outcome will be. That's why investors who are at or near retirement should consider instituting a downturn defense strategy. In the blink of an eye, a large portion of your retirement savings could vanish into thin air leaving you with few, if any, options. How would it feel if you had no other choice but to continue working well into your retirement years simply because a market crash robbed you of your retirement income?

The beginning phase of any successful retirement plan should start many years in advance. My first suggestion would be to start with something as simple as protecting your assets while they continue to grow inside your 401(k) plan just like we outline is this book. Additionally, for those savers who have monthly discretionary income they would be wise to contribute to a guaranteed compounding instrument to multiply their compounding efforts even further. The secret to accumulating significant wealth is to start as early as possible, stay consistent, and eliminate or minimize losses.

> The famous investor **Warren Buffet** says, "Never go backwards." Listen to him, he knows!

You don't need millions to make millions; you just have to have a fundamentally sound plan. The sun always shines brighter when the correct measures are taken to help minimize losses because that's where the magic of compounding begins. In very simple terms, think about the compounding effect of forming a snow ball and rolling it downhill. The snow ball becomes bigger and bigger and eventually rolls itself down the hill effortlessly. The hardest part of compounding is to start by setting it into motion.

Stay consistent with a plan over time; it will start to grow and multiply at very meaningful rates. The rewards of steady unshakable discipline will be very gratifying in the end. The *You* many years from now will be very proud of the self-discipline you exercised to hold the line and stay consistent by saving a little today for your bright sunny future of tomorrow.

Protecting your assets at any stage in life is without question one of the most responsible and important elements to your wealth building strategy. We all remember how the market crashes in 2000-2003 and 2008 created 12 years of lost opportunity cost for millions of Americans. During that time period, many people who were about to retire were forced to alter their retirement in some way or not retire at all and just continue working. A word of caution would be not to leave your financial future open to chance. You have worked too long and too hard to let it all evaporate overnight. No one thought the 2000 and 2008 crashes would happen to them, but it did and it was devastating for millions of Americans retirement accounts.

People have told me they are scared to death about losing large amounts of their retirement dollars, but yet they have not taken the appropriate steps to protect their investments. I have found when it comes to personal finances some people have become paralyzed by conflicting information which makes it hard for them to be confident in their decisions. Others are living in a state of denial by thinking "*it won't happen to me*". There is also a hesitation among some consumers because they fear being taken advantage of or manipulated. And before they will let that happen, they decide to roll the dice, hope for the best and do nothing!

Living in the 21st century by default is a very uncertain and complicated time. Severe market losses, rising health care costs (Medicare +7% annually), the whispers of potentially higher tax rates, and Social Security falling apart are on everyone's mind. Once upon a time, the fear that Social Security would disappear seemed more like an urban myth than a realistic scenario. However, there is serious talk in Congress and catastrophic financial predictions that Social Security (and Medicare) will indeed be reduced or even cease to exist for future generations.

Our financial future and well-being are hanging in the balance. Unless we make some forward looking decisions today, our financial health tomorrow could certainly become very questionable. Planning early is a key element to retirement success. Many folks are taking action today to protect their future tomorrow. I believe someday, history will be very kind to these forward looking planners.

So when it comes to finding the right financial professional, I believe that person should be someone you enjoy spending time with. Feeling comfortable with the person you are trusting with your life savings is a big deal. In fact, my recommendation for every retiree is to carefully assemble a team of trusted professionals to provide leadership and guidance in all areas of retirement life.

This thing we are calling retirement is going to be the longest and most expensive vacation of our lifetime. Having contingency plans in place to help deflect or at least reduce the financial burdens of unexpected emergencies is critical to your retirement success. So, if you really want to have a great retirement, there needs to be a lot of focus towards risk management in order to get there. Building an A-Team around you for the future will help reduce stress and instill confidence by knowing you are walking into retirement with trusted professionals by your side.

I suggest you only work with a Fiduciary advisor. Why? The financial service industry is a very crowded space with a lot of different companies and brands. Those companies and brands put enormous pressure and sales requirements on their advisors to sell what they have to offer. I know this because I started my career at one of those large firms. These firms only follow the suitability standard which means as long as it's suitable, they can sell it to you.

A Fiduciary is an Independent Advisor who is bound by the duty of law to safeguard your interest above all others including their own. They have only one loyalty and that is to their client's well-being and financial success.

We were all born with a certain level of discernment and intuition that serve us well throughout life. When you find the right person to provide leadership and guidance for your financial dealings, you will know. But clearly, you must take the time to do your own research and put forth the effort to find the person you feel most comfortable with. The hardest part in choosing the right financial advisor is just like many other things in life; it requires taking the first step. But once you do and you put in the time and efforts necessary, I believe you will find the right person to provide the highest level of client care and leadership for you.

CHAPTER 12

IRA & 401 (k) Rollovers

Successful and Unsuccessful people do not vary greatly in their abilities.
They vary in their desires to reach their potential.

– John Maxwell

If you are currently near retirement age you are part of the 78 million strong Baby Boomer generation. There are 10,000 Boomers reaching retirement age every day and like the millions of retirees before you, there are major decisions coming your way. Just remember, that your retirement will be the longest and most expensive vacation of your life. Being able to walk into retirement with confidence and peace of mind is priceless and for many people, it resembles a badge of honor and the excellence of accomplishment. Simply put, planning for your dream retirement many years in advance is a very wise decision and one you will never regret.

One of the most powerful early planning techniques proactive pre-retirees use to their advantage can only be done at a certain age. **59 ½** is a magical number. Here's why.

At **59** ½ you become eligible to exercise the In-Service-Rollover provision in your employer-sponsored plans while you are still working. In-Service Transfers to an IRA give you the opportunity to protect the Principal from Market Losses. The other major benefit to using an In-Service-Rollover is that the Plan Participants can continue to contribute to their retirement plans after an In-Service Rollover and receive employer matching funds giving you the best of both worlds. This can be accomplished by transferring a portion of your assets into Insurance based instruments. There are literally hundreds to choose from and this is one area where I have seen people select products that are not best suited for their needs. So take your time and make sure you understand how they function and why they benefit your situation better than all the others out there. Another area of concern would be putting too much money into a single product. When you take the time to strategically map out your tax burdens along with your income needs, you can create the flexibility needed for navigating your way in an unknown future tax environment. Generally, that flexibility requires the use of multiple accounts. While it takes a little more time to initially set up, the rewards in an uncertain future could be well worth a little extra time today.

Additionally, while these monies are growing in a safe and guaranteed a mid-single digit rate of return environment, you can still contribute to your 401(k) plan and enjoy the same advantages like employer matches and tax deductions you previously enjoyed. To be clear, when you exercise the

In-Service-Rollover, your 401(k) account can remain open for future contributions.

It's like getting across the finish line safely ahead of the pack. This opportunity also opens up so many additional options to the employee that can potentially enhance their retirement savings. Having the ability to reduce or completely eliminate market risks erases uncertainty before you retire. This is a big stress reliever that can put pep in your step and bring more confidence and peace of mind to your life. In addition to mitigating high fees and high risks, the use of safe indexing strategies designed for continued growth of your principal is a good option to consider as well.

> The famous investor **Warren Buffett** calls inflation **A Cruel Tax.**
>
> Let's not forget what **Albert Einstein** famously said, *Compound interest is the eighth wonder of the world. Those who understand it, earn it. Those who don't, pay it!*

This is worth repeating. After the In-Service-Transfer is complete, the employee can still continue to contribute to the same employer sponsored plan and continue to receive employer matching funds and tax deduction benefits until they retire. And the in-service rollovers can be accomplished without fees or taxes of any kind. Everyone who can exercise this safe money management strategy should take a careful look at how the In-Service-Transfer could benefit them. This type of savvy money management enables the employee to utilize the power of compound interest and the safety of principal while they continue to build their wealth without market risks and excessive fees. Exercising the In-Service-Transfer can help protect your hard earned money and bring about a sense of relief in knowing what you worked so hard to accumulate over your lifetime is now safe and all yours! During your retirement, every dollar counts so plan carefully!

There is no rule that says you have to roll the entire amount inside your 401(k) to one location. Take your time and work with a fiduciary advisor to make the most of your financial future. A smart mathematically correct solution in this area will ensure that you receive the necessary income increases to outpace inflation, but also keep your taxable income within certain thresholds to steer clear of severe penalties. Depending on your type of investments and their taxable characteristics, separating them into multiple locations can provide great flexibility. In this ever- changing world, having all your assets lumped into a single location could severely limit your options or leave you with no options.

A mathematically correct solution would strategically position assets to accomplish specific functions. For example, your advisor would help you determine your total net after tax income needs. Proportional amounts of monies would be assigned for essential daily living needs, long term care needs, recreational or vacation funds, charitable or legacy planning, continued growth, and an emergency fund account that gets replenished when necessary by the growth monies.

Assets that are set aside for growth purposes can continue to build wealth while you spend down your assets to ensure you will never run out of money. Having a sufficient emergency cash position to deal with unforeseen life events removes the stress of large unexpected cash expenditures. Mathematically correct strategies will replenish what you spend as it continues to regenerate itself over and over.

Pre-retirement planners should also take a careful look at the possibility for higher taxes in the future and select advisors and planners that offer tax exempt solutions for portions of their retirement income. Simple logic and mathematics tell us that 28 trillion dollars (and rising) in U.S. national debt is a very heavy lift to repay and it's going to fall on the backs of hard working Americans like you and me. How you position your savings today could become very beneficial many years from now when the tax rates could be significantly higher. On the other hand, if no meaningful tax strategy is formulated, there could be substantially less income for you to spend in retirement due to a higher than expected tax bite.

There should always be a defined goal in mind when selecting a home for your 401k rollover. This is also one area that requires thoughtful and careful examination and oversight. Your financial advisor should explain the pros and cons of each location or portfolio to you so you can make the very best decision.

If you are married and both of you have 401(k) accounts, your odds of outpacing inflation just got a lot better. Obviously, two incomes are better than one, however couples can potentially utilize some or all of one retirement account for daily essential living expenses and in a mathematically correct, tax efficient and guaranteed way. Then the couple can strategically assign some of one spouse's assets for growth and future emergencies. This can help your odds of never running out of money and you will get periodic income increases along the way plus you get to plan the level of increases you would like and at what time periods you receive them. That type of plan flexibility is designed to remove stress and boost confidence for retirees but it takes some work to get there.

The In-Service-Transfer can create multiple opportunities for growth, safety of principal and compounding opportunities and when handled properly new doors can open for a much brighter future to emerge. Unknown future tax rates could significantly impact our retirement lives so how we position our assets today will determine our spendable income tomorrow. Planning your retirement for unforeseen events like LTC needs, Inflation and potentially higher tax rates can help smooth out the longest vacation of your life.

Make no mistake about it you are the keeper of your retirement kingdom and unless you pay really close attention to what's going on around you today, you could experience some pretty severe self-inflected obstacles later on that you may never be able to overcome in retirement. There are no do-overs here so please take this seriously. Look at this as your last opportunity to save yourself from complete financial disaster in your retirement years.

It's also very important to work with an advisor who is in no way conflicted by their association or loyalty to any institution which could compromise their fiduciary responsibility to the consumer. Many investors unknowingly get financial guidance from an adviser who, while knowledgeable, may only represent a specific firm and its proprietary financial products. That advisor may also be getting paid an undisclosed commission to sell that specific firm's proprietary products, which may not be the best products available for you.

Unfortunately, these non-fiduciary advisers are often placed in the challenging position of serving their clients while also achieving the goals of their company. This means that there is an inherent conflict of interest for this adviser. These advisers are required to offer "suitable and appropriate" products but "suitable and appropriate" is quite broadly-defined. This is called a broker's representative suitability standard. However, they are usually not legally bound to do what is in the best interest of each client.

The suitability standard opens the door to conflicts of interest, which may not be disclosed to the client. The bottom line is that the non-fiduciary adviser's primary loyalty is usually to his or her company, not to you, the client. As an Investment Adviser Representative *(IAR)*, I am legally required to put your interests first. I am YOUR Fiduciary. I take your financial well-being and our relationship very seriously. When you work with me, your peace-of-mind is my number one goal.

In today's world, some words are thrown around loosely and many words have lost their true meaning. The word "Fiduciary" happens to be one of those words. Many advisors claim that label, yet some do not honor the true standard required of it. So, how do you know who is a Legal Fiduciary? The only *"Legal Fiduciary"* is an IAR or Investment Adviser Representative. IAR's work for RIA's or Registered Investment Advisors. CFPs are not Legal Fiduciaries but rather Professional Fiduciaries. The IAR could go to jail if they swindled you. If a CFP did the same thing, they would face disciplinary actions like being fined or barred from practicing. So, the Legal Fiduciary (IAR) has a lot more at stake when it comes to representing your best interest.

CHAPTER 13

Auntie IRMAA

What the government gives, it must first take away.
— John S. Coleman

Auntie IRMAA is Uncle Sam's wife. IRMAA (Income-Related Monthly Adjusted Amount) is the latest way the government plans to recover those *future tax dollars* you and I agreed to pay when we started our traditional 401(k) plans. Everyone is excited when they start contributing into their 401(k) plan and they give little thought to future taxes and no one could have imagined legislation like (IRMMA) would be passed. The retirements of millions of Americans who were financially responsible and accumulated wealth are now the target of a government in desperate need of more tax revenues. We all agreed to defer paying taxes on our 401(k) contributions to a later date sometime in the future at an unknown tax rate. A nice chunk of the 34.9 Trillion dollars Americans have saved for retirement could help patch a big hole in the sinking ship. The day of reckoning is near and it's looking pretty scary.

There is *Income* and there is *IRMAA Income*. The IRS keeps track of all of this too. They compute your adjusted gross income + any tax-exempt interest or EVERYTHING on lines 2a and 8b of your 1040 tax return and use that for their calculations. Remember, tax rates are fluid and congress has the power to increase them at will.

Sadly, the coveted employer sponsored Tax-Deferred 401(k) plans that we thought were going to be our main retirement income source is now being raided. The advice of many pundits, talking heads, and even some financial advisors in the past was that *taxes should be lower in our retirement years.* Well, Should be and will be are very different realities. Thirty trillion dollars in national debt has consequences for all of us. But only after you retire and become dependent on the government for your health care will you get to see the real cost of your health care.

For those of us who have become numb to these gigantic numbers and their impact, I would like to put into prospective how much ONE TRILLION DOLLARS actually is. *If you were to spend a million dollars every day from when Jesus walked the earth until today, year 2021, you would have only spent about $738 billion dollars. That's well short of a trillion dollars and less than 1/30th of our 30 trillion dollars of projected debt according to the CBO.* Currently millions of Americans are following the advice of uninformed advisors which will lead to this IRMAA tax grab ending very, very badly for millions unless they seek a way around it.

When rolling over your qualified plans, you should be keenly aware of how your future income is going to be impacted regarding your Social Security Medicare Surcharges. Many advisors today have no knowledge or understanding of the Income-Related Monthly Adjusted Amount (IRMAA). In the future, traditionally designed retirement income plans are going to be severely penalized according to the level and sources of income. We hear a lot about the phrase, *The New Normal,* being thrown around. IRMAA is here to stay and I suspect the surcharges will increase as well because Medicare has been rising at approximately 7% for years now. There is the potential that some Social Security checks could be eaten up by Medicare Surcharges leaving the retiree little or even nothing to live on. I have seen these projections and it is nothing less of horrifying.

This could be one of the biggest shocks retiree's face in their lifetime. In my opinion, this "Will Be" the biggest unexpected shock retirees face in their lifetime. Sadly, no one in government, no one in the news, and only a limited few financial advisors are paying attention to this tax train barreling down the tracks straight towards ALL of us. It's critically important that you understand how severe these coming surcharges will be so you can prepare accordingly. You will need to work closely with an advisor who has the expertise to fully illustrate the damaging effects this new and very discrete tax law will have on your assets.

Remember, this has absolutely nothing to do with your health or medical history. The *Income-Related Monthly*

Adjusted Amount (IRMAA) is aimed directly at those with certain classifications of retirement incomes. The more one makes and the more one has saved the more one pays in Medicare Surcharges. That is especially bad news for middle class income earners because these surcharges will be more damaging to their ability to save or spend in retirement. Your assets are now factored into the equation increasing the tax burden.

Sources of Retirement Income that will trigger Medicare Surcharges

➢ Social Security
➢ Wages
➢ Pension Income
➢ Rental Income
➢ Specific Annuities
➢ Traditional 401(k)
➢ Traditional IRA's
➢ Traditional 403 (B)
➢ Traditional 457
➢ Traditional SEP-IRA
➢ RMD
➢ Capital Gains
➢ Dividends (Including municipalities)

Sources of Retirement Income that do not trigger Medicare Surcharges

- ➤ Roth Accounts (Employer & Individual)
- ➤ Certain Life Insurance Policies
- ➤ Specific Annuities & Annuity Strategies
- ➤ Certain Long Term Care Policies
- ➤ Health Savings Accounts (HAS's)
- ➤ 401 (H) plans
- ➤ Home Equity

The IRS totals these sources of income for determining your Medicare Surcharge (Tax). The more you make through the trigger sources of income, the more you pay. That's why accurate retirement income planning is so important. If you overlook something this critical, your retirement income could be severely compromised. Additionally, because of the tax liabilities involved, many people will choose to spread the re-allocating of these sources of income over a multi-year time frame. A tax professional experienced in this area will help you minimize these tax burdens.

Imagine being in your golden years and you abruptly learn that your lifetime of disciplined and calculated savings has now put you in a position that takes away your social security income because you saved too much. Most likely, what you are reading is upsetting and in fact, you may find it pretty unbelievable. I understand how you feel because I too was upset and unbelieving when I first learned the plans the government has already set into motion.

You should work with an advisor who has knowledge of IRMAA and also has the resources to run your own personal calculations. Once you see for yourself the dollar amounts you will be forced to pay for government healthcare (Medicare) under the Affordable Care Act, the sooner you will understand how serious IRMAA is. It's hard to imagine that the income we were all counting on from traditional 401(k) plans has become ticking time bombs for the elderly.

CHAPTER 14

Summary

"There is a powerful driving force inside every human being that, once unleashed, can make any vision, dream, or desire a reality."

— Anthony Robbins:

Plan Providers and Third-Party Administrators avoid giving investment advice to plan sponsors. As a result, many plan sponsors need help guiding their employees through the maze of investments inside their plan. My goal in writing this book was to bring business owners and their employees closer together by revealing many of the untold truths lurking inside of traditional 401(k) plans. Helping employees properly position themselves to face many retirement obstacles they are currently unaware of sets the table for a closer relationship between the two.

A good word to describe how employees will feel by learning these untold truths is grateful. After all, the employer is providing their employees with a retirement savings tool that many employees are just winging. Some employees are currently guessing at which investments to choose simply because they have no professional investment guidance to lean on. That could very well be a liability issue waiting to happen soon after the next stock market crash.

I hope you learned something new from this book. If you feel the urge to take proactive steps to improve your retirement and those of your employees, I applaud you for that decision. The excitement and enthusiasm that can result from business owners providing their employees with this level of leadership can be a very powerful and rewarding experience for business owners. Touching the human spirt in a way that says *"I care about you and your family's financial security"* is one of the richest experiences I have felt in my lifetime and you can experience it too.

Business owners understand their moral, legal, and fiduciary obligations surrounding their 401(k) plans and many are eager to delegate some of those responsibilities. Because business owners are focused on their day to day operations, trying to carve out enough time to teach their employees about their investment options can be a very difficult and daunting task. Helping employees select their investments also comes with a certain degree of liability. Reducing that liability requires finding a qualified Section 3(38) Investment Manager who has a proven system in place that is easy to use and seamless to integrate into their existing 401(k) platform. I represent such an Investment Manager who has a 20-year history of keeping clients on the right side of the market.

In just a few easy steps, I show plan sponsors and their employees how to effectively utilize their plans (2R or SDBA option). When all of the 401(k) investments are handled by Section 3(38) Investment Managers, by default, the plan sponsors liabilities shrink as a result. The benefits of using advanced technology combined with active daily management to oversee your 401(k) plan will help you keep pace with today's lightning fast investment world. Without it, your 401(k) is simply a sitting duck in a vast ocean of volatility and risks. That is the same type of risk and volatility that tore millions of 401(k) accounts in half at the beginning of this century.

As of this writing June 2021, 401(k) accounts are at or near their highest levels ever. Real Estate is at or near its highest levels ever. US debt is at its highest level ever having reached an astonishing $28 Trillion dollars and it's expected to exceed $30 Trillion dollars by the end of the year. Our government's unfunded liabilities stand at a staggering $148 Trillion. 22% of all US dollars were printed in the last year. The total US Federal Debt to Gross Domestic Product (GDP) ratio stands at 143%. Much of America is struggling to stay afloat and COVID has left all of us full of anxiety. Could something possibly trigger another market crash or financial crisis?

Why not chart a course towards a safe harbor so you and your employees can relax knowing your retirement future is being carefully monitored by professionals that have a track record of keeping their clients on the right side of the market. Knowing you have a team of professional money managers whose primary function is to safely reposition your investments in times of crisis and also take advantage of new market uptrends is now in vogue for thousands of Americans. Having the right balance of offense and defense is what most investors lack today, but that can change for you very quickly the moment you embrace the 401(k) revival.

About the Author

"There are three kinds of people in this world - those that make it happen, those that watch it happen and those that wonder what in the heck happened."

        – Philosopher, Friedrich Nietzsche

Michael Watkins has been a serial entrepreneur most of his adult life. Having employed over fifty people in the 1980's and 90's, Michael is attuned to people's desire to improve their quality of life and financial stability. He also understands how difficult it can be to work a job, raise a family, get ahead, enjoy life, and save for the future all at the same time.

Michael has worked inside the financial services industry for over a decade and has seen a reoccurring theme when helping his clients plan for their dream retirement; *many account balances have been woefully inadequate to support the retirement dreams for which many people were hoping.* I knew most of my clients' problems stemmed from the two market crashes at the turn of the century which essentially wiped out half of their life savings. That's what I knew, but I didn't know how to fix it. Then in 2020, we were in the middle of a worldwide pandemic and a lot of things got shuffled around for me and millions of Americans. It was during this time of change and discovery that the fix fell directly into my lap.

I instantly knew I could help thousands or even millions of hard-working Americans and so here we are today embarking on that journey. I wrote *The 401(k) Revival* to help usher in the type of 401(k) leadership everyday investors need in order to build the wealth necessary to fund a 20 plus year retirement income. I am very confident that today's 401(k) investors will do significantly better than the previous generations when they employ risk management and other forward looking strategies I outline in the book.

Still Have Questions?

IF you still have questions or would like to guard your employee's retirement savings from the potential of a severe market crash or even the help of my team for you and your employees to avoid the retirement traps I outline in this book, contact me.

Contact me directly @ mwatkins@tampabayadvisory.com or 813-854-4400.

To get a private look at your future Social Security/Medicare Surcharge Burden, email me @ mwatkins@tampabayadvisory.com with your request for a consultation call.

You may also visit www.tampabayadvisory.com or www.The401kRevival.com

Acknowledgements

Thank you Jesus for molding and shaping what I gave you.

My mother, Martha Francis Thompson,
for giving me life and teaching me the Golden rule.
I miss you every day Mom!

My wife Annie for being my rock, soulmate,
and biggest cheerleader. *I Love You!*

Drew Horter for giving me the perfect platform to
work from.

Matt DiMaio for inspiring me to write this book.

Vance Howard, Cole Staton, and Steve Allbritton with
Howard Capital Management for contributing. Thank you!

My advisor brethren; Rick Miller, Scott Weldon, Dean
Statler and T-Bone.

Clestine "The Purpose Coach" and the *All-Women's
Workshop"* I somehow ended up in. Your inspiration was a
God wink to me. clestine@mypurposecoach.com

Jason Grantz with American Trust for your contribution

Tom Mishoe, CPA for your contribution
tom.mishoe@gmail.com

Deb Corey for helping me with ME!
healthywithdeb@gmail.com

My publishing team; Eli (The Book Guy)
eli@elithebookguy.com and
Maryellen O'Rourke @ AA Printing,
maryellen@printcentral.com

Brook Borup and the "My Clone Solution Team" for all the
website and techie love, brook@myclonesolution.com

To you the reader—I hope this information will
bless your life over and over.

79465515R00075